CATHOLIC LAITY

IN THE MISSION OF THE CHURCH

CATHOLIC LAITY
IN THE MISSION OF THE
CHURCH

RUSSELL SHAW

REQUIEM PRESS
BETHUNE, SC
2005

No part of this book may be reproduced or transmitted in any form, or by any means, electronic, mechanical, photocopying, or otherwise, without the prior written permission of the publisher, except by a reviewer, who may quote brief passages within a review.

Cover Artwork: 'The Sower' by Jean-François Millet
Image ©Sterling and Francine Clark Art Institute, Williamston, MA

REQUIEM PRESS
P.O. Box 7
Bethune, SC 29009
1-888-708-7675
www.RequiemPress.com

ISBN 0-9758542-8-3

Library of Congress Control Number: 2005928074

Printed in the United States of America

Contents

I.

THE LAITY FROM APOSTOLIC TIMES THROUGH THE MIDDLE AGES

Are we living in the age of the *laity*[g]? People sometimes call it that. But there is much hard work to be done before Catholic lay women and men universally recognize, accept, and carry out the role in the Church's mission that is theirs by right and obligation—and before others truly recognize that they should. The aim here is to help in bringing these things about.

We can begin by asking ourselves what a genuine age of the laity ought to look like. Some people seem to think it would mean more lay ministry and/or more power sharing with the clergy. Increased lay participation in decision-making in the Church is indeed a worthy goal, as is—up to a point—involving more lay people in *ministry*[g]. We shall say a lot more about both things below.

But an age of the laity that went no further than power sharing and ministries would not, in the final analysis, amount to much. The story of Gianna Beretta Molla suggests what an age of the laity that deserved the name might truly be like.

---

[g] - words noted with this superscript are defined in the Glossary.

Gianna was born October 4, 1922, near Milan. She studied medicine at the University of Milan and the University of Pavia, graduating in 1949. A specialist in pediatrics, she gave herself generously as a doctor to the poor, joined Catholic Action, and met an engineer named Pietro Molla, whom she married in 1955. She was a woman who enjoyed skiing, going to the opera, playing the piano, and puttering with oil paints.

Pietro and Gianna had three children. After several miscarriages, in 1961 Gianna Molla was pregnant again.

Toward the end of the second month she started experiencing sharp pain. The diagnosis was a fibrous tumor of the ovary. As a doctor, Gianna knew the score: either a hysterectomy that would kill her baby or surgery that would spare the child but leave her own life at risk. She chose the latter. "Save the baby," she told her husband and her physician.

Gianna Emanuela was born April 21, 1962. Soon her mother began to experience severe pain from septic peritonitis. She died on April 28, 1962. "Jesus, I love you," were her last words.

Pope John Paul II beatified her April 24, 1994, and on May 16, 2004, declared her a saint. Her husband and children were present at the ceremony. In his homily at the Mass of canonization the Pope said: "The extreme sacrifice she sealed with her life testifies that only those who have the courage to give of themselves totally to God and to others are able to fulfill themselves." The priest who promoted her canonization cause called her death "the culmination of a life lived with great intensity and a profound love of God and her fellow man."

And that, at the heart of it, is what a genuine age of the laity would be all about.

Even now, of course, there is plenty to celebrate. Not so long ago, nobody would even have thought of speaking of "the age of the laity." An episode in the career of John Henry Newman, the eminent nineteenth-century British Catholic convert and theologian, suggests the view of laity prevalent then.

Today, Newman's *On Consulting the Faithful in Matters of Doctrine* is regarded as a careful, nuanced discussion of one means at the disposal of the *Magisterium*[g] for ascertaining the faith of the Church. "The body of the faithful," Newman pointed out, "is one of the witnesses to the fact of the tradition of revealed doctrine." People take that for granted now.

It was different in 1859, when Newman's essay first appeared. A fierce controversy followed publication, with Newman himself in its center. This painful episode would dog him for years to come.

Some members of the British clerical establishment took Newman's essay as an assault on authority and its author as a dangerous troublemaker. Several years after the essay was published, one of them wrote to Archbishop (later, Cardinal) Henry Edward Manning of Westminster: "Dr. Newman is the most dangerous man in England, and you will see that he will make use of the laity against your Grace."

And the prominent lay people who supported Newman? The writer expressed his contempt in these words: "What is the province of the laity? To hunt, to shoot, to entertain? These matters they understand, but to meddle with ecclesiastical matters they have no right at all." It was a joke—the kind that speaks bitter truth.

Thinking about the role of lay people in the Church has come a long way since then. Especially notable progress was achieved at the Second Vatican Council (1962-65) and during the pontificate of Pope John Paul II. Yet every serious student of this subject realizes that serious problems and uncertainties of both a theoretical and practical nature persist, while new ones have emerged in recent years. Newman's vision of Catholic lay people who know their faith, are deeply committed to it, and strive enthusiastically to live it out is still far from universally realized.

The fundamental aim of what follows is to help realize it. In *On Consulting the Faithful* and other works, Newman often took a historical approach, shedding light on the present from the experience of the past. Adopting something of the same approach here, we begin this examination of the role of the Catholic laity in the mission of the Church by taking a quick look at history. This overview will touch on a few highlights of a long, complex story stretching over two millennia.

The Early Church

In a number of places in the New Testament we find the Apostles assigning functions of various kinds to their early collaborators, including lay people. In one way or another, these functions all replicate and express the threefold ministry of Christ as prophet, priest, and king.

At the same time, though, it is important to be aware that the New Testament offers no support for the view that in these early times all members of the Christian community were essentially the same from the point of view of ministry. Referring particularly to the celebration of the Eucharist, a historian of the priesthood says:

> The view that the New Testament indicates that the total community was enjoined to celebrate the Eucharist, so that in principle any baptized Christian might be the eucharistic celebrant, appears to be totally without any foundation.... Ministerial leadership in general is the basis for eucharistic leadership in particular (Kenan B. Osborne, O.F.M., *Priesthood: A History of the Ordained Ministry in the Roman Catholic Church*. Mahwah, N.J.: Paulist Press, 1988, p. 80).

Still, at the start the sociological and ecclesial distinction between clergy and laity was not so strongly emphasized as it came to be later. The terms "priest" and "layman" are not even found in the New Testament as names for distinct classes or categories of persons within the Christian community. One reason why *priest* is not used to refer to a certain group of men may have lain in the early Christians' desire not to seem to be taking anything away from the unique priesthood of Christ (cf. Heb 10.12). But we can also see another reason at work. There was a strong sense in these early days of the unity and fundamental equality of all members of the Christian community, interacting within a hierarchical structure that provided for a number of complementary roles and functions.

Another historian describes the situation existing in the first three centuries this way:

> Presbyteroi [priests] and even some episkopoi [bishops] continued to live as ordinary working men, tending their farms and businesses. Only in case of need did the local episkopos subsidize the presbyter. In most respects, sociologically, the presbyter was not differentiated from the lay person (Alexander Faivre, *The Emergence of the Laity in the Early Church.*Mahwah, N.J.: Paulists Press, 1990, pp. 144-45).

The vision of the Church as a hierarchically structured communion of fundamentally equal persons with complementary roles, working together to build up and sustain the whole, is memorably expressed in St. Paul's metaphor of the *Mystical Body of Christ*[g]. In his first letter to the Corinthians—a community that was, it seems, torn by conflicts that threatened to reduce it to competing factions— he begins by emphasizing the unity and equality of all.

11

> Now there are varieties of gifts, but the same
> Spirit; and there are varieties of service, but the
> same Lord; and there are varieties of working, but
> it is the same God who inspires them all in every
> one. To each is given the manifestation of the Spirit
> for the common good (1 Cor 12.4-7).

Warming to his theme, Paul turns to the image of the body as a vivid illustration of what he has in mind. "For just as the body is one and has many members, and all the members of the body, though many, are one body, so it is with Christ," he writes.

> For the body does not consist of one member but
> of many. If the foot should say, "Because I am not
> a hand, I do not belong to the body," that would
> not make it any less a part of the body. And if the
> ear should say, "Because I am not an eye, I do not
> belong to the body," that would not make it any
> less a part of the body....If all were a single organ,
> where would the body be? As it is, there are many
> parts, yet one body....But God has so composed
> the body, giving the greater honor to the inferior
> part, that there may be no discord in the body, but
> that all the members may have the same care for
> one another.

Hammering his point home in reference to the Christian community—in Corinth and everywhere else—Paul then declares:

> Now you are the body of Christ and individually
> members of it. And God has appointed in the
> church first apostles, second prophets, third
> teachers, then workers of miracles, then healers,

helpers, administrators, speakers in various kinds
of tongues (1 Cor 12.12-28).

For our present purposes, the message could hardly be more
clear: Lay people are full members of this body of Christ, the
Church, quite as much as anybody else, and in that capacity
the laity have important work to do.
In writing of the roles of members of the Christian
community, St. Paul's emphasis is upon what they do *within*
the Church in order to build her up and be of service to one
another. They are healers, helpers, administrators, speakers
in tongues, and so on. Within a fairly short time, however, the
realization grew that, by reason of their membership itself,
the Christian community's lay members also were called to
accept their share in doing the work of the Church precisely
by what they did *outside* the confines of the ecclesial
community. That is to say, they were called to be
evangelizers—by their very manner of life, to give witness to
the world regarding their faith.

This momentous idea is stated with great clarity and
force in a famous work of Christian apologetics called the
Epistle to Diognetus. Composed around the year 200 AD, it
is cast in the form of a letter to a high-ranking Roman official.
Of the Christians it says in part:

> Yet while they dwell in both Greek and non-Greek
> cities, as each one's lot was cast, and conform to
> the customs of the country in dress, food, and mode
> of life in general, the whole tenor of their way of
> living stamps it as worthy of admiration and
> admittedly extraordinary....In a word: what the
> soul is in the body, that the Christians are in the
> world....The soul, when stinting itself in food and
> drink, fares the better for it; so, too, Christians,
> when penalized, show a daily increase in numbers
> on that account. Such is the important post to

which God has assigned them, and they are not at liberty to desert it (*Epistle to Diognetus*, in Colman J. Barry, O.S.B., ed., *Readings in Church History*. Westminster, Md.: Christian Classics, 1985, pp. 39-40).

Plainly, this, too, refers to the lay members of the Church quite as much as it does to her clergy. It is not just the clergy who build up the Church and evangelize the world by causing the light of faith to shine forth in their lives. And if the realities of Christian life in those early days often were—as may well have been the case—rather less glorious than the glowing ideal set out in the Epistle to Diognetus, that in no way takes anything away from the fact that this truly *was* the ideal.

Unfortunately, it was not to remain that.

The Clericalization of the Church

As times and circumstances changed, in the Church and in the world, so thinking and practice concerning clergy and laity also changed. This is to say that *clericalization*ᵍ set in.

The process began around the beginning of the third century AD—that is, not so long after the Epistle to Diognetus was written. More and more emphasis came to be placed upon the difference between *clerics*ᵍ and lay people. The clergy increasingly became a religious elite, more or less isolated from ordinary lay life. At the same time, the laity gradually came to be looked upon—and also to look upon themselves—as being essentially passive in religious affairs.

A number of different factors worked together to bring about this change. Let's look at some.

The ecclesiastical policy of Constantine and his successors. Attributing military triumph over his rivals to the will of the Christian God, the Emperor Constantine became a convert to Christianity in the year 312 AD. He then set out vigorously to protect, promote—and direct—the fortunes of the religion he had embraced.

There was nothing unusual about this. Indeed, it was consistent with the common understanding of a Roman emperor's role at a time when there was no separation of church and state as we understand it now, and the emperor was regarded as being supreme not just in the religious sphere as well as the civil, secular one. We should not be surprised, then, to find Constantine referring to himself as the Church's "bishop of external affairs."

The clericalization of the Church was part of the religious policy pursued by Constantine and his successors. Their intention may have been to make clear the sacred nature of the Christian priesthood in contrast with pagan priests who customarily were regarded as state functionaries. Clerics now were exempted from civil and military service, from being answerable to civil courts, and from the payment of taxes. Visible differences between clergy and laity grew more and more pronounced, with distinctive garb and the *tonsure*[g] becoming common among clerics. Church councils in the fifth and sixth centuries further underlined the lay-clergy separation by insisting that ordination was irrevocable—once a cleric, always a cleric. Increasingly, too, the priesthood was limited to unmarried men.

In line with developments like this, the approach to public worship also changed. The *liturgy*[g], formerly understood to be an action in which the people actively participated, more and more became something that priests did while the people simply watched.

The rise and spread of monasticism[g]. The monastic movement was well underway by the fourth century AD. By no means was it limited to clerics and religious at the start, since lay people also were drawn to this mode of living, spiritually and physically removed from the world, that embodied a more demanding, intense way of serving God than ordinary, everyday life. Gradually, however, ordination became the rule for men in monastic communities.

One result was that lay people came to be thought of as less religiously serious and spiritually elevated than those who embraced the monastic way of life. And, predictably, this thinking eventually was applied outside the monastic context, as the monastic model became normative for clerics generally.

Summing up what happened, the theologian Yves Congar writes: "The lay condition is presented as a concession to human weakness....From the Christian point of view life in the world is a compromise....The laity, concerned in temporal affairs, have no part in the sphere of sacred things" (Yves Congar, O.P., *Lay People in the Church*. London: Geoffrey Chapman, 1985, pp. 12-13).

The influence of St. Augustine and his interpreters. St. Augustine of Hippo (354-430) is one of the towering thinkers in Christian history. But he does play a role in the story of the laity's decline. Especially when taken over by lesser interpreters who came after him, Augustine's radical emphasis on fulfillment in the next world and his de-emphasizing of life in this one tended to devalue the way of life of even devout Christian lay people.

The consequences can be seen centuries later in a volume like the enormously influential fifteenth-century spiritual masterpiece *The Imitation of Christ.* Marvelous work that it is, it nevertheless abounds in sayings like this: "Unless a man be detached from all created things, he cannot freely attend to spiritual things" (*The Imitation of Christ,* II, 21). But that, it might be said, is difficult advice for a lay person to carry out who believes conscientious and well-ordered concern for many different "created things" to be not only unavoidable for human beings but an important part of what it means rightly to attend to the things of the spirit!

But it would be wrong to suppose that either then or later the Church failed in its fundamental duty to form lay people for life in heaven or that lay people as a group failed massively in their fundamental duty to be so formed. The gospel was preached, the sacraments were administered, lay women and men for the most part lived decent, productive lives leading to fulfillment in eternal life. Still, the view of the laity and the temporal order that then prevailed was of little help to this ever-so-important project; at times, it may actually have been more or less a hindrance.

The Middle Ages

The socially and politically chaotic situation that followed the collapse of the Roman Empire accelerated the decline in the laity's status in several ways. The religious and cultural level of the barbarians who were the new Christian converts often was far inferior to that of the clerics who had evangelized them; and as time went by, the general eclipse of learning which spread through Europe only made matters worse. Clerics were very nearly the only educated people around, and even they often were semi-educated at best.

In this era, too, conflicts between lay lords and the clerical hierarchy became a continuing fact of life. The tension was rooted in the common failure—so visible in the case of a ruler like the all-powerful Constantine—to distinguish between church and state and the rights of the authorities in each sphere. By the seventh and eighth centuries, lay lords commonly controlled not only the property of the Church but the selection of bishops, abbots, and parish priests. The portioning-out of religious offices became a political power game whose painful, predictable result was that those selected often were unworthy of the offices they held.

The system as a whole is referred to by the expression "*lay investiture*[g]." Putting an end to lay investiture and correcting abuses in clerical life were central goals in the reform movement that arose at the French Benedictine monastery of Cluny in the tenth and eleventh centuries and was especially associated with Pope Saint Gregory VII (1073-1085). Although Gregory's lengthy conflict with the Emperor Henry IV ended with the Pope's death in exile, his determined assertion of papal authority in the face of imperial claims eventually bore fruit.

The *Cluniac reform*[g] movement made for a stronger papacy, a stronger clergy, and a healthier Church. But it also had an unintended result—fostering clericalization and weakening the position of the laity in the Church.

New theological and popular thinking about the priesthood and the Eucharist also played their role in this development. Increasingly, the celebration of the Mass became an action of the priest separated from the people. "The Mass was now believed to produce spiritual benefits whether or not it was devoutly attended....By the end of the Middle Ages, the Mass had been transformed from an act of public worship into a form of clerical prayer" (Patrick J. Dunn, *Priesthood: A Re-examination of the Roman Catholic Theology of the Presbyterate*. Staten Island, N.Y.: Alba House, 1990, p. 85). The popular piety and Eucharistic devotion which flourished at this time are indeed among the glories of medieval Catholicism; but encouragement given to the religious passivity of the laity is not.

The static, highly-structured character of feudal society in the late Middle Ages also contributed to a situation in which active roles in the mission of the Church were reserved for the clergy. Lay people were expected to be passive and docile in religious affairs. Few grasped the fundamental idea of personal vocation—that God calls each member of the Christian community to play a unique role in carrying out his redemptive plan.

What this meant as a practical matter can be seen in the case of a committed Christian like *St. Thomas More*[g]

(1478-1535). After concluding that, contrary to what he had for years hoped and more or less supposed was the case, he was not called to be a monk, the young More faced a serious personal crisis. "Since marriage was a mere concession to weakness, it was certainly not a path to perfection—or so held the cultural prejudice of More's age. Therefore, when this young, brilliant, idealistic youth struggled to accept what eventually emerged as a clear call to marriage, he was brought almost to the 'very gates of hell'" (Gerard B. Wegemer, *Thomas More: A Portrait of Courage*. Princeton, N.J.: Scepter Publishers, 1995, pp. 10-11).

Thomas More was exceptional but in this matter he was not unique. One writer sums up the situation of the laity like this:

> In the Middle Ages the layman found his field of action reduced to worldly affairs, with the disappearance of the sense of the laity's active participation in the field proper to the Church, which had been so lively in the early centuries; the Church's mission came to be identified almost exclusively with the ministry of the clerics, and Christian perfection came to be considered as something proper to clerics and religious. The layman's possibilities were reduced to the practice of the common virtues in the exercise of his secular functions, which was generally presented in ascetic literature as an obstacle to the Christian life of perfection (Alvaro del Portillo, *Faithful and Laity in the Church*. Shannon, Ireland: Ecclesia Press, 1972, p. 17).

With the advantage of half a millennium's hindsight, we can see now that change was needed. It soon came—but not easily or painlessly. It began with that huge fracturing of Christendom called the Reformation.

Spiritual Treasure

Christians spend their days on earth, but hold citizenship in heaven. They obey the established laws, but in their private lives they rise above the laws. They love all men, but are persecuted by all. They are unknown, yet are condemned; they are put to death, but it is life that they receive. They are poor, and enrich many.

Epistle to Diognetus, c. 200 AD

II.

THE LAITY FROM THE REFORMATION TO MODERN TIMES

Here we shall move very rapidly from the fifteenth century all the way to the early twentieth century. In both the secular and religious spheres profound changes of many kinds marked this enormously complex and crucial span of nearly half a millennium, which usually is called the "modern" age. Unfortunately, we cannot pause to examine them in detail. Instead we must concentrate on high points that concern our subject: the role of the laity in the mission of the Church.

Along with all the other changes in these centuries, changes in thinking about the laity also took place. On the whole, though, these were less pronounced than the changes in other sectors of secular and religious life. The old view of the Catholic laity—as more or less passive recipients of the ministrations of the clergy and persons who sought, and were expected to seek, a lower level of spiritual excellence than priests and religious—tended to persist.

This corresponded to the prevailing image of the Church as a kind of pyramid, with the pope at the top, bishops, priests, and religious on descending levels, and the lay faithful—far and away the largest number of Church members, of course—at the bottom. Cardinal Avery Dulles, S.J., describes the "unfortunate consequences in Christian life" that tended to flow from this way of thinking.

> While some virtues, such as obedience, are strongly accented, others are not....Clericalism tends to reduce the laity to a condition of passivity, and to make their apostolate a mere appendage of the apostolate of the hierarchy.... Juridicism tends to exaggerate the role of human authority and thus to turn the gospel into a new law. Catholics in the Counter Reformation period became overly concerned with fulfilling ecclesiastical obligations and insufficiently attentive, at times, to fulfilling the law of charity. Concerned with maintaining the right relationships with pope and bishops, they attended less than they should to God, to Christ, and to the Holy Spirit (*Models of the Church*. New York: Doubleday Image Books, 1978, page 48).

At least in this area, the modern age witnessed more continuity in thinking with the medieval past than it did change.

Yet new ideas about lay people and their role now and then did appear. They can be found here and there in the writings of people like St. Ignatius Loyola, St. Francis de Sales, Jean Pierre de Caussade, S.J., and John Henry Newman. Although the new ideas did not immediately produce large-scale practical results, they did help set the stage for many of the significant developments that have occurred in our times.

The Reformation and Ordinary Life

But instead of starting with these Catholic thinkers, we need to begin with Martin Luther and the early Protestant reformers, and with their ideas about the value of ordinary life.

The feudal society of the high Middle Ages was, as we saw, highly structured and stable. With but few exceptions,

22

people were locked from birth on into the same social class, occupation and way of life, and even geographical locale that their parents and parents' parents had occupied for many generations. In a society where there was little or no social mobility, there were relatively few major 'vocational' choices to make (except, perhaps, by people considering becoming priests or nuns), nor was there much sense of personal vocation. The ordinary life of the laity was not held in high esteem, nor were ordinary lay people.

Profound change set in with the end of the Middle Ages. The rigid hierarchical structure of medieval society gave way to new economic and political systems. With heightened openness to social mobility and change, people had an increased sense of personal option. Old thinking that stressed the superiority of a hereditary aristocracy was challenged by a growing affirmation of the value of ordinary life—the way of life of the vast majority of the laity.

The new thinking is associated especially with Martin Luther and the *Reformation*[g]. As these early Protestants saw it, it was a contradiction in terms to speak of Christians as being more or less committed, since total commitment to the gospel was an obligation for all. No longer was the serious pursuit of excellence in Christian life limited to a clerical and religious elite. The Christian laity, too, were called by God to the pursuit of Christian excellence in the context of their everyday lives.

This was a valid and important insight. Unfortunately, Luther and his followers carried it too far—to the repudiation of "*mediation*[g]" in the realm of spiritual life and, along with this, of certain major elements of Christian faith and life as they had been traditionally understood. According to their understanding, the philosopher Charles Taylor points out, faith itself

> seemed to require an outright rejection of the
> Catholic understanding of the sacred, and hence

also of the church and its mediating role….Along with the Mass went the whole notion of the sacred in medieval Catholicism, the notion that there are special places or times or actions where the power of God is more intensely present and can be approached by humans….The rejection of the sacred and of mediation together led to an enhanced status for (what had formerly been described as) profane life. This came out in the repudiation of the special monastic vocations which had been an integral part of medieval Catholicism (Charles Taylor, *Sources of the Self: The Making of the Modern Identity*. Cambridge: Harvard University Press, page 216).

Along with rejecting mediation and ordained priesthood, the Reformation embraced *congregationalism*[g], including the belief that the *priesthood of the faithful*[g] which comes from baptism is sufficient to empower someone to celebrate the Eucharist and the other sacraments. In this view, the true celebrant is the congregation, not an ordained minister; and the congregation can designate whichever of its members it chooses to preside.

Of course, there is a kernel of truth in this, for as Vatican Council II taught, in participating in the celebration of the Eucharist, the faithful "offer themselves to God and themselves along with it" (*LG* 11). But Vatican II also underlined the crucial fact that baptismal priesthood and ministerial priesthood "differ essentially and not only in degree" (*LG* 10). The congregationalist approach reduces the all-important distinction to the vanishing-point, with a resulting confusion of clergy and lay roles.

Pope John Paul II reaffirmed the truth of faith involved here in his encyclical "On the Eucharist in its Relationship to the Church," *Ecclesia de Eucharistia*, which he published in

2003. Speaking of the "distressing and irregular" situation of a Christian community that lacks a priest, he said:

> Parishes are communities of the baptized who express and affirm their identity above all through the celebration of the Eucharistic Sacrifice. But this requires the presence of a presbyter, who alone is qualified to offer the Eucharist *in persona Christi*[g] (*Ecclesia de Eucharistia*, 32).

Not surprisingly, the extreme views of the early Protestants had the effect of discouraging Catholics from pursuing what was good and worthwhile in their new thinking concerning the laity and lay life.

Other things also contributed to this result. For instance, the Council of Trent (1545-1563), convoked to organize the Catholic response to the challenge of the Reformation, played a role in what happened. By any reasonable standards, Trent's positive achievements were immense. But while giving close and much-needed attention to reforms in clerical life, the Council said almost nothing about the laity and their role. This silence tended to reinforce and institutionalize the inferior position occupied by lay people in religious affairs.

> The institutional, hierarchical aspect of the Church received all the attention, and the ordinary faithful were left in the shadows. With all this concentration on ecclesiastical authority and the hierarchy, it was inevitable that the Church would be seen as the domain of the clergy (Jordan Aumann, O.P., *On the Front Lines: The Lay Person in the Church After Vatican II*. Staten Island, N.Y.: Alba House, 1990, p. 8).

25

But despite that, important Catholic voices now and then took a significantly different line. Let us turn now to what some of them said.

Some Catholic Thinkers on the Laity

One of the outstanding figures of the Catholic Counter-Reformation launched in response to the Protestant Reformation was St. Ignatius Loyola (1491-1556), founder of the Society of Jesus or Jesuits. Composed to help people discern and accept their vocations, the *Spiritual Exercises* of this highly disciplined former military man make it clear that God addresses his call both "to all" and "to each one in particular" (*Spiritual Exercises*, 95). Moreover, God does not call people only to the priesthood or religious life; he also summons others to serve him as lay persons in the world. Each individual must discern God's will for himself or herself, and act accordingly.

St. Ignatius writes:

> I must not subject and fit the end to the means, but the means to the end. Many first choose marriage, which is a means, and secondarily the service of our Lord in marriage, though the service of God is the end. So also others first choose to have benefices [hold clerical positions with an established income], and afterwards to serve God in them....As a result, what they ought to seek first, they seek last.
>
> Therefore, my first aim should be to seek to serve God, which is the end, and only after that, if it is more profitable, to have a benefice or marry, for these are means to the end. Nothing must move me to use such means, or to deprive myself of them, save only the service and praise of God our

Lord, and the salvation of my soul (*Spiritual Exercises*, 169).

Significantly, Ignatius's *Spiritual Exercises* sometimes were given to lay people. The great spiritual writer and bishop St. Francis de Sales (1567-1622) aims his *Introduction to the Devout Life* specifically at the laity and argues that holiness is a genuine possibility and an obligation for people in the world. Declaring that God commands "all Christians…to bring forth the fruits of devotion, each according to his character and vocation," he calls it "an error, or rather a heresy, to try to banish the devout life from the regiment of soldiers, the shop of the mechanic, the court of princes, or the home of married folk" (*Introduction to the Devout Life*, translated and edited by John K. Ryan. New York: Doubleday Image Books, 1955, pp. 39-40).

But St. Francis goes even further than that in his *Treatise on the Love of God*, published in 1616. Here he deals at length with the unique, unrepeatable calling to a particular role in the divine plan that each baptized individual receives from God.

Like Ignatius of Loyola, Francis de Sales maintains that it is not God's intention that everyone live a life organized by the *evangelical counsels*[g] of poverty, chastity, and obedience. Rather, God wants people to undertake "only such counsels as are suitable according to differences in persons, times, occasions, and abilities."

The counsels, after all, are for the benefit of the Christian community as a whole, not for its members as individuals. "There are circumstances that make them sometimes impossible, sometimes unprofitable, sometimes dangerous, and sometimes harmful to certain men…. Charity is the rule and measure of their fulfillment," St. Francis insists

(*Treatise on the Love of God*, volume II. Rockford, IL.: Tan Books, 1975, pages 70-71).

And, much as Martin Luther might have done, St. Francis also underlines the crucial importance of a person's particular calling, typically found in the circumstances of daily life.

St. Francis de Sales' teaching on personal vocation and vocational discernment applies as much to lay people as to those called to be clerics or religious. So does his succinct advice for recognizing the authenticity of a vocational discernment: "The three best and surest marks of lawful inspiration are perseverance in contrast to inconstancy and levity, peace and gentleness of heart in contrast to disquiet and solicitude, and humble obedience in contrast to obstinacy and extravagance" (*Treatise on the Love of God*, volume II, page 92),

Among Catholic thinkers of these centuries, none is more important for what he says about the laity in the Church than John Henry Newman (1801-1890), the distinguished British convert to Catholicism who did pioneering theological work on a many different topics and themes. Earlier, we referred to the controversy that greeted the 1859 publication of his essay *On Consulting the Faithful in Matters of Doctrine*. Let us now take a closer look at what Newman actually says there.

In seeking to ascertain the age-old faith of the Church on particular questions, he argues, the pope and the bishops— that is, the Magisterium or teaching authority of the Church— do well to determine what the body of the faithful believe. This does not mean deciding what the Church should teach by staging referenda or conducting opinion polls or conditioning acts of magisterial teaching on prior consultation with the laity. Newman's point is both more subtle and more authentically Catholic than that.

By way of illustration, Newman cites what happened during the *Arian heresy*[g] of the fourth century: Although many bishops departed from faith in the divinity of Christ, the body of Catholic laity, remaining "faithful to its baptism," stood by this central doctrine of Christian faith. So also, he points out, in times far less troubled than the fourth century, Pope Pius IX just a short time before had consulted widely on the state of Catholic belief regarding the *Immaculate Conception*[g] before solemnly defining that Marian dogma as a matter of faith in 1854.

What is one to make of episodes like this? Newman writes:

> Though the laity be but the reflection or echo of the clergy in matters of faith, yet there is something in the *"pastorum et fidelium conspiratio"* [agreement of pastors and faithful], which is not in the pastors alone....Pope Pius has given us a pattern, in his manner of defining, of the duty of considering the sentiments of the laity upon a point of tradition, in spite of whatever fullness of evidence the Bishops had already thrown upon it (*On Consulting the Faithful in Matters of Doctrine*. New York: Sheed & Ward, 1961, pp. 103-104).

The truth of this is commonly taken for granted today.

We also should bear in mind something else Newman says, at the conclusion of the essay. Quoting a historian's description of the people's enthusiastic response to the announcement that the *Council of Ephesus*[g] in 431 AD had declared that Virgin Mary was rightly called *theotokos*— Mother of God—he writes:

> My own drift is somewhat different from that which has dictated this glowing description; but

the substance of the argument of each of us is one and the same. I think certainly that the *Ecclesia docens* [teaching Church] is more happy when she has such enthusiastic partisans about her as are here represented, than when she cuts off the faithful from the study of her divine doctrines and the sympathy of her divine contemplations, and requires from them a *fides implicita* [implicit faith] in her word, which in the educated classes will terminate in indifference, and in the poorer in superstition (*On Consulting the Faithful*, p.106).

This is a powerful plea for those in responsible positions to do what it takes to ensure that the Church has educated, informed lay members.

To a remarkable degree, Newman also anticipated the idea of personal vocation, which, as we have begun to see—and will see at still greater length later—is so important to a correct view of the Christian lives of the laity and all other members of the Church. We find a particularly notable treatment of this subject in one of the sermons, "Divine Calls," which Newman preached while still an Anglican clergyman.

Without summarizing all of it, let us consider one passage that gives the flavor of the whole:

For in truth we are not called once only, but many times; all through our life Christ is calling us. He called us first in Baptism; but afterwards also; whether we obey His voice or not, He graciously calls us still. If we fall from our Baptism, He calls us to repent; if we are striving to fulfil our calling, He calls us on from grace to grace, and from holiness to holiness, while life is given us. Abraham was called from his home, Peter from his nets, Matthew from his office, Elisha from his farm, Nathanael from his retreat; we are all in course of calling, on and on, from one thing to another, having no resting-place, but mounting towards our eternal rest, and obeying one command only to have another put upon us. He calls us again and again, in order to justify us again and again,—and again and again, and more and more, to sanctify and glorify us ("Divine Calls," *Parochial and Plain Sermons*. San Francisco: Ignatius Press, 1987, pages 1569-1570).

Newman makes it clear that he is not speaking only of the clergy. He includes in what he says all members of the Church at every stage in their Christian lives. Christ's particular will for each one comes "through our natural faculties and circumstances of life." This way of proposing and revealing our vocations to us is "in all essential respects what His voice was to those whom He addressed when on earth" (page 1570).

The Catholic Laity in the United States

Things that were happening in the United States during these years also deserve a place in this story.

One of these, which was to be of central importance subsequently, was the prolonged struggle over a system of lay ownership of Catholic parishes called *lay trusteeism*[g]. It arose mainly in response to the circumstances of American civil law, but it also had other causes, including conflict between Catholic ethnic groups, the misapplication of American political principles to the Church, the influence of Protestant congregationalism, the rebellious actions of some priests, and the quarrelsome attitude of some lay people.

By the 1820s trusteeism had become a serious problem in places like New York, Philadelphia, Norfolk, and Charleston, S.C. Trustees claimed the right to veto bishops' pastoral assignments, recruit priests to their liking, and otherwise exercise control over the Church, under a separation-of-powers model resembling the American system of government.

Confronted with this challenge to their authority, the American bishops moved to eradicate the trustee system by civil and ecclesiastical means. Lasting until well into the middle years of the nineteenth century, the struggle placed a permanent stamp on lay-clergy relations in American Catholicism.

The other significant development occurred in the Diocese of Charleston where, in 1820, a newly arrived bishop, John England, sought to deal with the trustee problem by a policy of accommodating reasonable lay interests. The result was a constitution for the diocese (which at the time took in not only South Carolina but North Carolina and Georgia as well).

The Charleston constitution provided for vesting ownership of church property in diocesan trustees who included a lay majority chosen by lay people; electing lay vestrymen responsible for parishes' temporal affairs; and holding annual conventions of the Church in Charleston during which the clergy and laity made financial and other administrative decisions.

This unusual constitution remained in effect until Bishop England's death in 1842. When the Vatican was consulted, it said it saw no problems with what was happening in Charleston. Elsewhere, however, Church authorities, concerned with stamping out all vestiges of lay trusteeism, pursued a policy of rigid clerical and episcopal control over the property and affairs of the Church.

How things stood is clear in a homily preached on November 11, 1889 by Archbishop John Ireland of St. Paul, Minn., a leading figure among the U.S. bishops of the late nineteenth and early twentieth centuries, at an event celebrating the centenary of the establishment of the American hierarchy. "Let there be individual action," he urged. "Layman need not wait for priest...." But soon he got down to brass tacks: "Priests are officers, laymen are soldiers"; the laity should wait for their orders after all (quoted in Marvin R. O'Connell, *John Ireland and the American Catholic Church.* St. Paul: Minnesota Historical Society Press, 1988, page 283).

Despite visionary figures like Newman and John England, the situation in most places in the Catholic world during these centuries corresponded on the whole to the ecclesiological model assumed by men like Archbishop Ireland and earlier set out in the schema on the Church prepared for, though not acted upon, by the First Vatican Council (1869-70). The schema read:

> Christ's Church is not a society of equals as if all the faithful in it had the same rights; but it is a society in which not all are equal. And this is so not only because some of the faithful are clerics and some laymen, but especially because in the Church there is a power of divine institution, by which some are authorized to sanctify, teach, and govern, and others do not have this authority.

No doubt this is true of the Church in its institutional aspect. But it is a far cry from Paul's vision of a Church in which "to each is given the manifestation of the Spirit for the common good" (1 Cor 12.7)—as it is also from the vision that, less than a century later, was to emerge in the Second Vatican Council's teaching that the Church is Mystical Body of Christ, People of God, and *communio*—communion—which arises from and in some way reflects the divine-human communion of the New Covenant itself.

Spiritual Treasure

God has created me to do Him some definite service. He has committed some work to me which He has not committed to another. I have my mission. I may never know it in this life, but I shall be told it in the next. I am a link in a chain, a bond of connection between persons. He has not created me for naught. I shall do good; I shall do His work. I shall be an angel of peace, a preacher of truth in my own place, while not intending it, if I do but keep His commandments. Therefore, I will trust Him, whatever I am, I can never be thrown away. If I am in sickness, my sickness may serve Him, in perplexity, my perplexity may serve Him. If I am in sorrow, my sorrow may serve Him. He does nothing in vain.

John Henry Newman

III.

THE TWENTIETH CENTURY, THROUGH VATICAN II

Whatever else might be said for the early years of the twentieth century, they were surely not an "age of the laity." On the contrary, with the advantage of hindsight it is clear that this was an era when the Catholic laity occupied a secondary (or was it tertiary?) situation in the Church.

The Code of Canon Law published in 1917 illustrates the point. It was a remarkable achievement in many respects; but, of its 2,414 *canons*[g] (laws), very few concerned lay people. Apart from one canon saying the laity are entitled to receive the sacraments and another declaring that they may not wear ecclesiastical garb, most dealt with marriage questions.

The absence of the laity from the Code of Canon Law was not a result of simple oversight. It went much deeper than that. Bishop Alvaro del Portillo of *Opus Dei*[g] explains:

> The 1917 Code failed to pay adequate attention to the laity precisely because it would have been impossible for it to do so. There were no social manifestations sufficiently outstanding to claim legislative recognition; there was no juridical technique which could provide it; and there were no sufficiently sound theological bases which

could support any such provisions (*Faithful and Laity in the Church*, page 11).

Dismal as that may sound, Bishop del Portillo nevertheless adds that this nearly total absence of the lay faithful from the 1917 Code was "truly providential." Much preliminary work was required before anything useful could be said. Theological thinking had to mature. Decades of reflection and lived experience were needed before a reasonably satisfactory understanding of the laity could find expression in the Code of Canon Law or any place else. Indeed, it would be no stretch of the imagination to say that Vatican Council II had to take place first.

Already, though, the urgent need for this development was well on its way to being established by the alarming rise of secularization in Western society. The growing cultural power of secularization made dramatically clear the imperative need for the Church to find new ways of responding to this challenge.

Although the process had its roots in earlier events, the movement to drive the influence of faith from society came of age in the eighteenth century. Among the notable results of the elitist intellectual movement called the Enlightenment and the outburst of savage violence known to history as the French Revolution has been the continuing, self-conscious attempt to exclude religion from public life and allow it, at best, a barely tolerated role in the private sphere.

The adverse implications for lay women and men were significant. The Catholic philosopher Jacques Maritain speaks of the "spiritual impoverishment" of the laity, who in this way received further encouragement to believe that "the call to the perfection of charity, with what it implies of life of prayer and…of contemplative recollection, was the concern of the monks" (*The Peasant of the Garonne*. New York: Macmillan Paperbacks, 1969, page 59). Another result, flowing from this one, was the de facto exclusion of the laity from an active role in the apostolate—that is, a role in the mission of the Church.

Yet *secularism*'s[g] challenge to the Church also had certain very different results. So, for instance, there was a heightened sense that the laity would have to step in to fill the gap when it was clear (for example, during the anti-clerical violence of the French Revolution) that the clergy and religious alone could no longer carry on the work of the Church. The French Dominican preacher Henri Lacordaire (1802-1861) put it like this:

> The lay man has a mission to fulfil; he has to supply whatever may be lacking to the diocesan clergy and the religious orders, for their resources and for many means of action. Men of faith must join their efforts to defend truth against the ceaseless influence of evil teaching; their charity must work in common to repair the breaches in the Church and the social order (quoted in Congar, *Lay People in the Church*, page 360).

With hindsight, we can see that the way was being prepared for the major developments that were to take place during the first half of the twentieth century.

Catholic Action and Other New Thinking

For a long time, the most important of these was *Catholic Action*[g]. Although many Catholics today are unfamiliar with Catholic Action, until well into the middle years of the last century it was *the* officially-approved ecclesial organization harnessing the energies of Catholic lay people in the service of the Church's mission.

Popes strongly backed Catholic Action. Its fundamental purpose, said Pope Pius XI (1922-1939), who was sometimes called the Pope of Catholic Action for his championing of this movement, was "the formation of sincere Christians, who will know, love and live the Christian life in its integrity, showing that it is possible to fulfill perfectly the duties which it imposes on all classes, in every social and professional sphere." Many organizations, programs, and publications were established under Church sponsorship to pursue to this goal.

These years also witnessed the flourishing of the *liturgical movement*[g], which sought to bring about a renewal of the Church's public worship. Both in theory and in practice Catholic Action and the liturgical movement were closely linked. Both also were important in advancing the laity's cause.

So, for example, Dom Virgil Michel, O.S.B., a leader in the liturgical movement in the United States, wrote:

> All of us together, Christ and we, form a living spiritual body, the Church....The laity are not the clergy, priests are not bishops; yet we are all called to our active share in the life of Christ, that is, in the life of the Church, which is the mystic but real continuation of Christ. ("Significance of the Liturgical Movement," *N.C.W.C. Bulletin*, April, 1929)

Catholic Action, he added, was "but the further development of the liturgical life...we must have the liturgical life before we can have true Catholic Action."

But Catholic Action was hobbled by built-in limitations. Chief among these perhaps was the repeated insistence that Catholic Action was, in the words of Pope Pius XI, "the participation of the laity in the apostolate of the Hierarchy." In other words, in participating in Catholic Action, Catholic lay people were not engaging in an apostolate properly theirs—not doing something they had a right and duty to do just because they were members of the Church—but were sharing in something that properly pertained to the clerical hierarchy. Thus Catholic Action was sometimes said to be the "long arm" of the bishops, whereby the laity, working under the bishops' direction, would carry out the hierarchy's policies in sectors of society otherwise beyond its reach.

Even so, Catholic Action was not the only model of *lay apostolate*[g]. In time, new groups appeared that saw the participation of the laity in the Church's mission as something that came from being members of the Church. These groups, which included Opus Dei, Focolare, and secular institutes, anticipated a form of organized lay apostolate that Vatican Council II later would specifically endorse.

During these years two encyclicals by Pope Pius XII also played an important role in the development of new thinking about the laity.

In *Mystici Corporis* (1943), Pope Pius presented a vision of the Church based on St. Paul's doctrine of the Mystical Body of Christ. This was an important step in the direction of what now is called *communio ecclesiology*[g]—a theology of the Church as a communion or community of persons and of local churches within the Universal Church. Pope Pius wrote that all Catholics, including the laity, have "the obligation of working hard and constantly for the upbuilding and increase" of Christ's Mystical Body (*Mystici Corporis*, 117).

In *Mediator Dei* (1947), Pius XII turned to the subject of prayer and worship. While insisting on the essential difference between the ordained priesthood and the priesthood of the faithful, he also declared that lay people participating in the celebration of the Eucharist are not passive spectators but active participants. This is true "in two ways," he wrote: "namely, they offer the sacrifice through the hands of the priest and, to a certain extent, they offer it together with him" (*Mediator Dei*, 92). This expressed central insights of the liturgical movement while anticipating key principles of the liturgical reform prescribed by Vatican II.

Another landmark publication was *Lay People in the Church*, a book by the French theologian Yves Congar, O.P., which first appeared in 1951. "Lay people will always be a subordinate order in the Church; but they are on the way to a recovery of a fuller consciousness of being organically active members thereof, by right and in fact," wrote the Dominican, whom Pope John Paul II named a cardinal in 1994. Congar grounded the "recovery of a fuller consciousness" by and about the laity in a new theology of the Church. "At bottom there can be only one sound and sufficient theology of laity, and that is a 'total ecclesiology'," he declared (*Lay People in the Church*, xi, xvi).

In these and other ways the stage was being set for the Second Vatican Council.

Vatican Council II

A full appreciation of Vatican II's view of lay people requires that we understand the purpose which Blessed Pope John XXIII had in view in convening the Council. In brief, he hoped to position the Church to deal with the phenomenon of *secularization*[g] by bridging the gap between the Church and the world that had grown alarmingly wide in recent centuries. In his document formally convoking Vatican II, Pope John put it like this:

> It is a question in fact of bringing the modern world into contact with the vivifying and perennial energies of the gospel—a world which exalts itself with its conquests in the technical and scientific fields, but which brings also the consequences of a temporal order which some have wished to reorganize excluding God (Apostolic Constitution *Humanae Salutis*, December 25, 1961).

But who are better situated to carry the gospel to the world than committed lay women and men, themselves full and active participants in the *secular*^g society in which they live and work as well as in the Church? Here was the central insight that shaped Vatican II's approach to the participation of the laity in the Church's mission, which was worked out over the four momentous sessions of the Council (1962-65) by the Catholic bishops of the world under the presidency of Blessed John XXIII and his successor, Pope Paul VI.

Among the fundamental questions for the Council was what attitude followers of Christ should to take toward the secular order. Vatican II's answer is stated in the opening sentences of its Pastoral Constitution on the Church in the Modern World, *Gaudium et Spes*[g]:

> The joy and hope, the grief and anguish of the men of our time, especially of those who are poor and afflicted in any way, are the joy and hope, the grief and anguish of the followers of Christ as well. Nothing that is genuinely human fails to find an echo in their hearts. (*Gaudium et Spes,* 1)

The Second Vatican Council is sometimes said to have reflected the secular optimism of the 1960s and taken an overly optimistic view of the world. While there are passages in *Gaudium et Spes* of which that may be true, the spirit of the pastoral constitution as a whole is not secular optimism but Christian hope.

The document is realistic about evils in the world, committed to seeking remedies in light of gospel values, and conscious that complete human fulfillment ultimately will be found not in this life but the next. The socio-political analysis of the pastoral constitution calls attention to the peculiar blend of light and shadow, progress and decline, typical of modern times. The Christian and eschatological dimensions of human affairs, and the close link between them, are expressed in passages like this:

> The Church believes that Christ, who died and was raised for the sake of all, can show man the way and strengthen him through the Spirit in order to be worthy of his destiny: nor is there any other name under heaven given among men by which they can be saved. The Church likewise believes that the key, the center and the purpose of the whole of man's history is to be found in its Lord and Master. She also maintains that beneath all that changes there is much that is unchanging, much that has its ultimate foundation in Christ, who is the same yesterday, and today, and forever. And that is why the Council…proposes to speak to all men in order to unfold the mystery that is man and cooperate in tackling the main problems facing the world today (*Gaudium et Spes,* 10).

This is not secular optimism but Christian faith and hope.

The pastoral constitution says Catholic lay people have an essential part in realizing the Church's commitment to serve the world. "It is to the laity, though not exclusively to them, that secular duties and activity properly belong….It is their duty to cultivate a properly informed conscience and to impress the divine law on the affairs of the earthly city….The laity are called to participate actively in the whole life of the Church… animate the world with the spirit of Christianity…be witnesses to Christ in all circumstances and at the very heart of the community of mankind" (*Gaudium et Spes,* 43). This remains a stirring challenge.

The scope and originality of the Second Vatican Council's teaching about lay people are most apparent, however, in two other documents: the Dogmatic Constitution on the Church, *Lumen Gentium*ᵍ, and the Decree on the Apostolate of Lay People, *Apostolicam Actuositatem*ᵍ.

As we saw above, *Lumen Gentium* is based on a *communio* ecclesiology that reflects the scriptural images of the Church as Mystical Body of Christ and, especially, People of God. The implications for Catholic lay people of this way of understanding the community of faith are profound. Vatican II insists that *all* the faithful, not just those who have been ordained or entered religious life, share in Christ's three-fold office as priest, prophet, and king (cf. *Lumen Gentium,* 10-13).

The most important element of the constitution's teaching on the laity is found in Chapter V, "The Call to Holiness." In earlier days, although lay people were expected to lead decent lives and save their souls, the common assumption was that, for practical purposes, the serious pursuit of a high level of sanctity was something for the clergy and persons in consecrated life. But *Lumen Gentium* teaches that "all Christians in any state or walk of life are called to the fullness of Christian life and to the perfection of love"; by the pursuit holiness, it adds, "a more human manner of life is fostered also in earthly society" (*Lumen Gentium,* 39).

"The forms and tasks of life are many but holiness is one," the Council declares. And, having applied this principle to bishops, priests, and deacons, it then speaks specifically of lay people:

> Christian married couples and parents, following their own way, should support one another in grace all through life with faithful love, and should train their children...in Christian doctrine and evangelical virtues. Because in this way they present to all an example of unfailing and generous love, they build up the brotherhood of charity....In a different way, a similar example is given by

widows and single people, who can also greatly contribute to the holiness and activity of the Church. And those who engage in human work...should rise to a higher sanctity, truly apostolic, by their everyday work itself (*Lumen Gentium,* 41).

Summing up, Chapter V underlines the central theme: "Therefore all the faithful are invited and obliged to holiness and the perfection of their own state of life." (*Lumen Gentium,* 42)

Hardly less important than Chapter V is *Lumen Gentium*'s Chapter IV, "The Laity." Here Vatican Council II teaches at length about the place lay women and men properly have in the mission of the Church.

The characteristic "proper and peculiar" to the laity, it notes, is secularity. This means that "by reason of their special vocation it belongs to the laity to seek the kingdom of God by engaging in temporal affairs and directing them according to God's will....[T]hey are called by God that, being led by the spirit to the Gospel, they may contribute to the sanctification of the world, as from within like leaven, by fulfilling their own particular duties" (*Lumen Gentium,* 31).

The dogmatic constitution contains a crucial affirmation of the equality-within-diversity which exists among all the Church's members. Alongside the variety of ecclesiastical offices and functions, it says,

there is a common dignity of members deriving from their rebirth in Christ, a common grace as sons, a common vocation to perfection, one salvation, one hope and undivided charity.....Although by Christ's will some are established as teachers, dispensers of the mysteries and pastors for the others, there remains, nevertheless, a true equality between all with regard to the dignity and to the activity which is common to all the faithful in the building up of the Body of Christ (*Lumen Gentium*, 32).

Lumen Gentium then turns to the laity's responsibility for *evangelization*[g]. Here it makes several key points:

*Lay people contribute to evangelization especially by their secular work in the world (*Lumen Gentium*, 36).

*The laity have a special responsibility for the conversion of secular culture and its structures and institutions (*ibid.*).

*Competent lay people possess the right, and sometimes the duty, to express their opinions to the pastors about matters pertaining to the good of the Church (*Lumen Gentium*, 37).

*Along with listening to the advice of lay people and giving them responsibilities in the Church, the pastors should encourage them to undertake initiatives on their own (*ibid.*).

Taking the teaching of *Lumen Gentium* as its basis and starting point, the Decree on the Apostolate of Lay People, *Apostolicam Actuositatem*, spells out practical implications of this body of ecclesiological doctrine.

The decree does not reject the Catholic Action model of lay apostolate (a participation in the apostolate of the clerical hierarchy which comes to lay people by hierarchical delegation), but goes beyond this model by setting out a much broader vision of the lay apostolate. In this view, the "right and duty to be apostles" come to lay people by "the fact of their union with Christ," specifically through baptism and confirmation (*Apostolicam Actuositatem*, 3).

Apostolicam Actuositatem strongly commends the "witness of life" of lay people—the testimony they give to Christian faith by the way they live their lives and do their jobs. At the same time, however, witness of life is "not the sole element" in lay apostolate; rather, "the true apostle is on the lookout for occasions of announcing Christ by word," both to unbelievers and also to other members of the Church (*Apostolicam Actuositatem,* 6).

The "fields of the apostolate" are said to include Church communities, especially parishes, the family, work with young people, and peer apostolate (*Apostolicam Acutuositatem,* 9-14). Individual apostolate is "the starting point and condition of all types of lay apostolate" (*Apostolicam Actuositatem,* 16). Christian social action is particularly important and involves a high degree of lay autonomy.

> Laymen ought to take on themselves as their distinctive task this renewal of the temporal order. Guided by the light of the Gospel and the mind of the Church, prompted by Christian love, they should act in this domain in a direct way and in their own specific manner. As citizens among citizens they must bring to their cooperation with others their own special competence, and act on their own responsibility (*Apostolicam Actuositatem,* 7).

Later, speaking of "group apostolate," the decree says that "while preserving the necessary link with ecclesiastical authority," lay people have "the right to establish and direct associations, and to join existing ones" (*Apostolicam Actuositatem,* 19). Catholic Action remains a praiseworthy vehicle of lay activity (*Apostolicam Actuositatem,* 20). But there should be no doubt: "In the Church are to be found...very many apostolic enterprises owing their origin to the free choice of the laity and run at their own discretion" (*Apostolicam Actuositatem,* 24).

Apostolicam Actuositatem makes provision for what today is usually called lay ministry:

> The hierarchy entrusts the laity with certain
> charges more closely connected with the duties
> of pastors: in the teaching of Christian doctrine,
> for example, in certain liturgical actions, in the
> care of souls. In virtue of this mission the laity are
> fully subject to superior ecclesiastical control in
> regard to the exercise of these charges
> (*Apostolicam Actuositatem,* 24).

But lay apostolate carried on in and to the secular world is the central form of lay participation in the Church's mission according to the Council's view of things.

Bishops and priests are urged to work diligently to promote lay apostolate and form lay people for it. At the same time, the clergy should bear in mind that "in the building up of the Church the laity too have parts of their own to play," and so "they will work as brothers with the laity" (*Apostolicam Actuositatem,* 25).

In this context, the decree calls for parish, interparish, diocesan, interdiocesan, national, and even international councils as bodies through which clergy, religious, and laity can collaborate in the Church's apostolic efforts. "These councils can take care of the mutual coordinating of the various lay associations and undertakings, the autonomy and particular nature of each remaining untouched" (*Apostolicam Actuositatem,* 26). Finally, the document calls for the establishment within the Holy See of a secretariat to promote lay apostolate (*Apostolicam Actuositatem,* 26). Today this agency is known as the Pontifical Council for the Laity.

Vatican II's teaching about the laity was a dramatic change from attitudes common in the not-so-distant past. Catholics in many cases still have a long way to go to internalize it and put it fully into practice. Along with the notable progress since Vatican II, there also have been discouraging setbacks.

Spiritual Treasure

The forms and tasks of life are many but holiness is one—that sanctity which is cultivated by all who act under God's Spirit and, obeying the Father's voice and adoring God the Father in spirit and in truth, follow Christ, poor, humble and cross-bearing, that they may deserve to be partakers of his glory. Each one, however, according to his own gifts and duties must steadfastly advance along with way of a living faith, which arouses hope and works through love.

Vatican Council II,
Lumen Gentium 41

IV.

AFTER THE SECOND VATICAN COUNCIL

The Second Vatican Council marks a great divide in the history of the Church in modern times. Standing on the far side of the divide, in the early years of the twenty-first century, we need to reflect on the post-Vatican II situation in the Church from the point of view of our theme: the laity in the Church's mission.

Many things, good *and* bad, have happened since the Council that have an impact on the role of lay people.

Positive developments at the topmost levels of the Church include the issuance in 1983 of a new *Code of Canon Law*^{g} for the Western Church, the 1987 general assembly of the world *Synod of Bishops*^{g}, which focused on the laity, and the publication of Pope John Paul II's Post-Synodal Apostolic Exhortation, *Christifideles Laici* (The Lay Members of Christ's Faithful People), dated December 30, 1988, and released January 30, 1989. Along with the Code of Canon Law and *Christifideles Laici*, we also shall look here at some problematical trends which emerged in the postconciliar years.

The Code of Canon Law

Vatican II and the new Code of Canon Law were linked from the start. On January 25, 1959, Blessed Pope John XXIII announced that he planned to convoke an ecumenical council. At the same time, he also announced a project to revise the compilation of laws for the Western Church. When the commission charged with this task finally met, Paul VI—pope by then—explained that Church law needed adapting to "a new way of thinking proper to the Second Ecumenical Council of the Vatican."

Unlike the earlier code of 1917, the 1983 code says a great deal about the laity.

The second of its seven books carries the title "The People of God." Its first part is "The Christian Faithful." Title I (canons 204-223) covers "The Obligations and Rights of All the Christian Faithful"; Title II (canons 224-231) deals with "The Obligations and Rights of the Lay Christian Faithful." An overview follows.

Obligations and Rights of All

Canon 204 notes that "Christian faithful" is a comprehensive term including all those who are incorporated into Christ in baptism and constituted the people of God. Sharers in Christ's priestly, prophetic, and kingly roles, they are called to "exercise the mission entrusted to the Church to fulfill in the world, in accord with the condition proper to each one."

Canon 205 identifies people fully in communion with the Church as those who are joined visibly with it in faith, sacraments, and governance, while canon 206 adds that the Church "already cherishes [catechumens] as her own." Canon 207 says the basic categories of Christian faithful are sacred ministers ("clerics") and laity, and, coming from among both groups, persons committed to the consecrated life of poverty, chastity, and obedience.

This is followed, in canon 208, by a statement with tremendous importance for the laity:

> In virtue of their rebirth in Christ there exists among all the Christian faithful a equality with regard to dignity and in the activity whereby all cooperate in the building up of the Body of Christ in accord with each one's own condition and function.

This declaration of equality-with-diversity is the fundamental principle of a new charter for lay people.

Coupled with it is the reminder, in canon 209, that the Christian faithful are obliged to carry out their obligations to the universal Church and also to their particular churches (dioceses). Canon 210 points out that "in accord with their own condition" all should seek personal holiness and promote the growth and holiness of the Church. Canon 211 affirms the duty and right of the faithful to engage in evangelization, the proclamation of the Good News.

Canon 212, in three parts, says the faithful: 1. are "bound by Christian obedience" to follow the teaching and decisions of the bishops; 2. are free to make their needs and wishes known to the pastors of the Church; and 3. according to their qualifications, have "the right and even at times a duty" to share their opinions about the good of the Church with its leaders and other Christian faithful, "with due regard for the integrity of faith and morals and reverence toward their pastors."

Canon 213 says the faithful have a right to receive from their pastors spiritual goods, "especially the word of God and the sacraments." Acknowledging the diversity of rites and spiritualities in the Church, canon 214 declares that Catholics can worship and pray in the approved manner appropriate to them.

The right of Catholics to establish and take part in charitable or religious associations or groups promoting the Christian vocation in the world is recognized in canon 215;

while canon 216 recognizes a similar right of Catholics to engage in apostolic action—although "no undertaking shall assume the name Catholic" without approval from Church authority.

Turning to education and the academic life, canon 217 says the faithful have the right to an authentic Christian education. Canon 218 upholds academic freedom, consistent with respect for the teaching authority of the Church and the rights of others, for those engaged in theology and other sacred disciplines.

Canons 219 and 220 recognize two bedrock rights—to choose one's *state in life*[g] without "any kind of coercion" and to enjoy one's good name and privacy. Canon 221 says all Catholics are entitled to be dealt with according to the norms of Church law; it also says they can defend their rights in a Church court (but, practically speaking, that is difficult or impossible for lay people to do except for marriage cases). Canon 222 says the faithful should support the Church, work for social justice, and assist the poor. Canon 223 declares that when acting either individually or in associations, Catholics should act with the Church's common good in view; it adds that Church authority can "regulate the exercise" of the rights of the faithful for the sake of this common good.

Obligations and Rights of the Laity

Having discussed obligations and rights of all Catholics, the Code of Canon Law turns next to certain specific right and duties of lay people. Title II of Book II covers these in eight canons, with the first, canon 224, simply saying that besides the rights and duties enumerated in the next seven canons, the laity have the rights and duties common to Catholics in general.

Canon 225 is long, complex, and important. It deserves to be quoted in its entirety:

1. Since the laity, like all the Christian faithful, are deputed by God to the apostolate through their baptism and confirmation, they are therefore bound by the general obligations and enjoy the general right to work as individuals or in associations so that the divine message of salvation becomes known and accepted by all persons throughout the world; this obligation has a great impelling force in those circumstances in which people can hear the gospel and know Christ only through lay persons.

2. Each lay person in accord with his or her condition is bound by a special duty to imbue and perfect the order of temporal affairs with the spirit of the gospel; they thus give witness to Christ in a special way in carrying out those affairs and in exercising secular duties.

Here is a mandate for lay apostolate and a brief statement of its program.

Canon 226 speaks of the duty of married Christians to work for the upbuilding of the Church through their marriages and family life. It also underlines the duty and right of parents to educate their children, and especially to provide for their religious education. Canon 227 affirms that the laity as citizens are free in regard to temporal affairs, though intrinsically obliged to act in the spirit of the gospel and in light of Church teaching. On questions legitimately open to different views they should not present their opinions as the position of the Church.

Canon 228 says qualified lay people can hold offices and perform functions in the Church open to them in Church law, and can also serve as experts or advisers to the pastors of the Church, "even in councils." Canon 229 says the laity should learn Catholic doctrine; can study in ecclesiastical universities and institutes and earn degrees in theology and related fields; and can receive official certification (a "mandate") to teach sacred sciences.

Repeating points made in a 1972 document of Pope Paul VI, canon 230 states that the ministries of *lector*^{g} and *acolyte*^{g} are open to lay men, and that lay people can serve as commentators or cantors and, if necessary, perform other functions like presiding at prayer services, conferring baptism, and distributing communion. Canon 231 notes that lay employees of the Church should be properly formed and should receive fair pay and benefits.

Here, then, is the heart of what the 1983 Code of Canon Law says about the rights and duties of Catholics as a whole and the Catholic laity in particular. It goes without saying that there are other duties and rights (many of them spelled out elsewhere in the code). Unfortunately, it also is a fact that practical means for upholding these rights are still lacking in many cases. Yet with all its limitations, intrinsic and extrinsic, this section of the 1983 code, like the teaching of Vatican Council II itself, marks a huge step forward for Catholic lay women and men.

Two Postconciliar Problems

Law is one thing, real life another. Despite the progress reflected in the Code of Canon Law, some serious problems have appeared in Catholic life since Vatican II. One of these is an error that the philosopher Jacques Maritain colorfully described as "kneeling before the world." Another is what is often called the clericalization of the laity.

Maritain's warning about kneeling to the world had special significance coming from him. Along with being one of the twentieth century's leading exponents of the thought of St. Thomas Aquinas, he had had a strong influence on Cardinal Giovanni Battista Montini—later, Pope Paul VI— and through him on the Second Vatican Council. Especially notable was his thinking about Christian *humanism*ᵍ and the duty of the laity to bring gospel values to bear on the secular order—ideas that were central to Vatican II's Pastoral Constitution on the Church in the Modern World, *Gaudium et Spes.*

Thus, in criticizing things he saw happening in the 1960s, Maritain was not expressing reactionary opposition to the Council. As one of the important intellectual influences who helped lay the groundwork for Vatican II, he was calling attention to serious distortions of its real meaning.

The 'Temporalization of Christianity'

In a book called *The Peasant of the Garonne*, first published in France in 1966, Maritain skewered Catholics' uncritical acceptance of the secular at the same time that anything smacking of traditional Christian asceticism or penance was being "automatically shelved as a matter of course." This strange and destructive behavior was very noticeable in regard to sex, where the human propensity for wrongdoing was systematically ignored, and in regard to social justice, which had become the almost exclusive preoccupation of some Christians.

Of such people, whom Maritain recognized as moved by "generous" intentions, he wrote:

> Instead of realizing that our devotion to the temporal task must be that much firmer and more ardent since we know that the human race will never succeed on this earth in delivering itself completely from evil—because of the wounds of Adam, and because our ultimate end is supernatural—they make of these earthly goals the truly supreme end for humanity (*The Peasant of the Garonne.* New York, Macmillan Paperbacks, 1969, pages 70-71).

The outcome to which all this tended, he warned, was the "complete temporalization of Christianity"—and, with it, the "temporalization" of Christians themselves.

Cultural Assimilation[g]

These problems not only persist today but in some ways have grown worse. Many Catholics in the United States and other Western countries have been assimilated into a secular culture shaped by values like individualism ('the right to choose' in regard to abortion, sexual behavior, and much else) and consumerism, which are in conflict with the values of the gospel. The focus is on getting results and gratifications in this world; the supernatural dimension of life is more or less ignored. The results can be seen in low rates of Mass attendance and participation in the sacramental life of the Church, the practice of contraception, abortion, and divorce among Catholics, and the phenomenon of 'pro-choice' Catholic politicians (Catholic political figures who without apology support legalized abortion and other practices contrary to Catholic doctrine).

Opinion polls repeatedly show that on many matters large numbers of lay Catholics either do not know what the Church teaches or do not care very much. "As we scan from the pre-Vatican II to the post-Vatican II generation," a sociologist says, "we find less and less attachment to the church."

Clericalization of the Laity

As for the clericalization of the laity, in *Christifideles Laici*, the apostolic exhortation which he issued after the synod on the laity, Pope John Paul explains that it exists among people who are "so strongly interested in Church services and tasks" that they neglect "their responsibilities in the professional, cultural and political world." Side by side with this error he discerns "separation of faith from life, that is, a separation of the Gospel's acceptance from the actual living of the Gospel in various situations in the world" (*Christifideles Laici*, 2).

Concern about clericalization today often focuses on the service roles in Church settings called lay ministries.

As we saw earlier, Vatican Council II assigned clear priority to the laity's task of bringing the message of Christ into the secular order—"the actual living of the Gospel in various situations in the world," as Pope John Paul puts it in the passage just quoted. At the same time, the Council indicated approval of *lay ministry*[g] ("the teaching of Christian doctrine, for example…certain liturgical actions…the care of souls": cf. *Apostolicam Actuositatem,* 24).

Lay ministry received a big boost in 1972 in a document of Pope Paul VI, *Ministeria Quaedam.* Along with abolishing "minor orders" and the subdiaconate, it assigned the functions of subdeacons to the lay ministries of lector and acolyte, while also inviting the emergence of other forms of lay ministry. "Ministries may be committed to lay Christians," Pope Paul said. "They are no longer to be regarded as reserved to candidates for the sacrament of Orders." (Strictly speaking, this is an analogical use of the term ministry. Ministry properly so-called is limited to the ordained; tasks entrusted to lay people are 'ministry' in an extended sense only.)

Since then, there has been an explosive numerical growth of lay ministries and lay ministers. This development is desirable in many ways. Increasingly, too, it has become a matter of necessity in many places, as the number of priests and religious has declined. By the late 1990s there were some 30,000 salaried lay ministers in U.S. parishes (although close to 30% of these 'lay' ministers were actually religious sisters or brothers); while an unknown, but obviously much larger, number of lay people served as volunteer Eucharistic ministers, lectors, and catechists.

Neglecting Lay Apostolate

Unfortunately, at the same time lay ministry was receiving strong encouragement and support from official Church sources, lay apostolate—the work of the laity in bringing the message and values of Gospel into the secular world—was largely ignored.

The results of this were summed up in a report to the Vatican (based on replies from dioceses), which the U.S. bishops' conference submitted in preparation for the world Synod of Bishops on the laity in 1987. To the question whether Vatican II's teaching on lay people was "welcomed, understood, and properly presented," the report said "three themes" stood out in the dioceses' replies.

> First, the conciliar teaching has been understood and welcomed where bishops and pastors have made serious, continuing efforts to present it; where these efforts are lacking, the teaching is not understood and appreciated.

> Second, while the number of lay people actively involved in some aspect of the Church's work has increased greatly since Vatican II, they constitute a small minority among the total number of laity.

> Third, lay participation is commonly understood as meaning involvement only in the programs and activities of the Church. Few lay people understand or are committed to the apostolate in the secular world (quoted in Russell Shaw, *To Hunt, To Shoot, To Entertain: Clericalism and the Catholic Laity*. San Francisco: Ignatius Press, 1993, p. 112).

As for positive results from the Council's teaching, the report pointed to the rise of lay ministries. Unfortunately, it said, there was "no corresponding increase in lay commitment to evangelization and the renewal of the temporal order."

The 1987 Synod and *Christifideles Laici*

The 1987 assembly of the world Synod of Bishops was held at the Vatican from October 1 to 30. Its theme was "Vocation and Mission of the Laity in the Church and in the World Twenty Years After the Second Vatican Council." Bringing together 232 bishops and other clergy as well as 60 auditors, most them lay people, this was the most extensive top-level discussion of the Catholic laity since Vatican II.

Pope John Paul summed up the assembly's deliberations and added his own thoughts in *Christifideles Laici*, "The Lay Members of Christ's Faithful People." *Christifideles Laici,* a form of papal document known as a Post-Synodal Apostolic Exhortation, was dated December 30, 1988, the feast of the Holy Family, and publicly released on January 30, 1989. It reaffirmed the teaching of Vatican Council II while expanding and updating it in significant ways.

The aim of the synod assembly, the Pope said, was that Catholic lay people play "an active, conscientious and responsible part in the mission of the Church in this great moment of history" (*Christifideles Laici*, 3). In particular, the laity have "an essential and irreplaceable role" in evangelization, for "through them the Church of Christ is made present in the various sectors of the world" (*ibid.*, 7).

The vocation of the laity does not come by delegation from the hierarchy, John Paul insisted. It comes from baptism and confirmation, and is theirs as members of the Church (*ibid.*, 14). The secularity of lay people, "a theological and ecclesiological reality," distinguishes them from clergy and religious (*ibid.*, 15). Called to holiness, they should make spiritual commitment visible "in their involvement in temporal affairs and in their participation in earthly activities" (*ibid.* 17).

The Pope discussed the role of laity in the Church in the context of Vatican II's *communio* ecclesiology. Each lay person has "a totally unique contribution" to make (*ibid.*, 20); "ministries and charisms" indicate what these contributions should be (*ibid.*, 20). Lay people can indeed render valuable service in Church institutions and structures. But certain mistakes must be avoided: "…a too-indiscriminate use of the word 'ministry', the confusion and the equating of the common priesthood and the ministerial priesthood, the lack of observance of ecclesiastical laws and norms, the arbitrary interpretation of the concept of 'supply', the tendency towards a 'clericalization' of the lay faithful and the risk of creating…an ecclesial structure of parallel service to that founded on the Sacrament of Orders" (*ibid.*, 23).

Christifideles Laici stressed the role of the laity in evangelization, including the re-evangelization of formerly Christian regions—for example, Western Europe—which have undergone secularization (*ibid.*, 34). Singled out for special attention was the apostolic role of lay women, especially their contribution to upholding the dignity of marriage and family life and "assuring the moral dimension of culture" (*ibid.*, 51).

John Paul further declared that the formation of Catholic lay people for apostolate should be a priority in every diocese. The fundamental aim of this formation should be to show the laity how to integrate their religious and secular lives. "There cannot be two parallel lives in their existence," the Pope wrote. "Every activity, every situation, every precise responsibility…are the occasions ordained by providence for a 'continuous exercise of faith, hope and charity'" (*ibid.*, 59).

The program of activity laid out in *Christifideles Laici* represents an enormous challenge to the resources of the entire

Church. Much work must be done to put it into practice—and, to a great extent, much that the document calls for has not even been attempted up to this time. In what follows we shall take a look at some things that need doing.

Spiritual Treasure

The whole Church, pastors and lay faithful alike, standing on the threshold of the Third Millennium, ought to feel more strongly the Church's responsibility to obey the command of Christ, "Go into all the world and preach the gospel to the whole creation" (Mk 16:15), and take up anew the missionary endeavor. A great venture, both challenging and wonderful, is entrusted to the Church — that of a *re-evangelization*, which is so much needed in the present world.

Pope John Paul II,
Christifideles Laici, n. 64

V.

THE PERSISTENCE OF CLERICALISM

Much of the program proposed for and to the laity by the Second Vatican Council and Pope John Paul II remains unaccomplished or only partly accomplished even now. One explanation for that lies in a persistent problem in Catholic life—*clericalism*[g]. It is not the only reason why the dreams of Council and Pope have not been realized, but it is one reason, and a very serious one.

Earlier, we saw the emergence of clericalism as a historical phenomenon; now we need to take a closer look at its essence as well as some of its current forms.

First of all, it is important to say that the clericalist mentality described here is not found in *all* clerics nor does it exist *only* in clerics. Countless Catholic lay women and men share the same assumptions and act upon them.

Clericalism, whether found among clergy or laity, assumes that clerics not only are but are *meant* to be the active, dominant elite in the Church and lay people the passive, subservient mass. As a result, the laity are discouraged, at least implicitly, from taking their proper share of responsibility for the Church's mission and evangelization is neglected. That includes neglecting the evangelization of culture—the effort to influence the structures and institutions of secular society so that they will reflect the values of the gospel. A large part of the vision of Vatican II remains unrealized as a result.

Clericalism intensifies the confusion about lay and clerical identity and roles that apparently is a factor in the morale problems of some priests. In this way it also deepens the vocations crisis in the Church in the United States and other Western countries. Although the clericalist mentality typically defines this crisis as a shortfall of new candidates for the priesthood and religious life, the crisis of vocations in its entirety also includes the apparent failure of many lay people not just to discern their vocations but even to give serious thought to the question of vocation. Clericalism likewise is a factor in the inappropriate political activity of some clerics. And it plays a part in the controversy over women's ordination.

Clericalism even can be seen at work in the scandal of clergy sex abuse. Not that clericalism causes sex abuse, of course, any more than sex abuse causes clericalism. But attitudes and ways of doing things associated with clerical elitism often took over when clerics were found to have engaged in abuse.

> How is it possible that bishops who, angry rhetoric aside, are known to be conscientious, intelligent churchmen made the horrendous mistakes some repeatedly made in dealing with wayward priests? The only credible answer to that question is that these bishops were acting according to the prevailing clericalist assumptions and procedures for handling priests who get into trouble: protect them to the point of coddling them, give them time off, therapy and new assignments, hush things up, keep knowledge of the mess confined within a very limited clerical circle....The clericalist culture is variously described as a caste system, a fraternity, a club. All of these terms fit. In part, clericalism

is the clergy's special mode of succumbing to two dangerous errors that threaten all professions: the perversion of solidarity among colleagues and low expectations with regard to professional responsibility (Russell Shaw, "Clericalism and the Sex Abuse Scandal," *America*, June 3-10, 2002).

Perhaps most serious of all, clericalism tends to discourage lay people from cultivating a spirituality that rises above a rather low level of fervor and intensity. As the clericalist mentality sees it, the serious pursuit of sanctity is the business of priests and religious. For the laity, Vatican II's universal call to holiness remains a muted trumpet: minimalistic religious practice and legalistic morality are all that is asked of many lay people—and all many ask of themselves, while the idea that the laity should, as a normal path, aspire to sanctity is dismissed as spiritual pretentiousness—"salvation in the fast lane," as a journalist once put it.

The Clericalist Dialectic

We need to be aware, however, not just of the harm done directly and visibly by the mentality of clerical elitism, but also of the destructive operation of a kind of clericalist *dialectic*[g]. It has produced a number of troublesome offshoots in reaction to the original abuse.

History is instructive on this point. The clericalist mentality in its political guise—a form of overreaching that usurps the role of the laity in the political order—helps account for the rise of European anti-clericalism in the eighteenth and nineteenth centuries. That is hardly surprising, since, as Yves Congar remarks, "forgetfulness of the true role of lay people leads both to clericalism in the Church and to *laicism*[g] in the world" (Yves Congar, *Lay People in the Church*. London: Geoffrey Chapman, 1985, page 53). This laicism has been marked—and today still is—by its fierce determination to exclude religious influence from public life and, in its most virulent forms, by overt or covert religious persecution.

*St. Josemaria Escriva*ᵍ, the founder of Opus Dei, once spoke of the problem of political clericalism this way:

> All those who exercise the priestly ministry in the Church should always be careful to respect the autonomy which a Catholic layman needs....To attempt the opposite, to try to *instrumentalize* lay people for ends which exceed the proper limits of our hierarchical ministry, would be to fall into a lamentably anachronistic *clericalism*. The possibilities of the lay apostolate would be terribly curtailed; the laity would be condemned to permanent immaturity; and above all, today especially, the very concept of authority and unity in the Church would be endangered (*Conversations With Monsignor Escriva de Balaguer*. Manila: Sinag-Tala Publishers, 1977, page 17).

Within the Church the dialectic of clericalism gives rise to other bad results. Notable among them is an exaggerated interest on the part of some laity and clergy in power-sharing arrangements of various sorts, based on the assumption that the advancement of lay people requires admitting them to offices and functions previously reserved for clerics—letting them look and act like priests. Lay ministries, for all that can and should be said in their favor, sometimes reflect this way of thinking.

St. Josemaria speaks of this dimension of clericalism, too, linking it to a "clerical sense" often given to the word Church itself—namely, "*proper to the clergy or Church hierarchy*." As a result, he adds, "many people understand participation in the life of the Church simply or at least principally as helping in the parish, cooperating in associations which have a mandate of the hierarchy, taking an active part in the liturgy and so on." But that is a mistake.

> I must insist that ordinary Christians can carry out their specific mission—including their mission in the Church—only if they resist *clericalization* and carry on being secular and ordinary, that is people who live in the world and take part in the affairs and interests of the world....The best and most important way in which they can participate in the life of the Church, and indeed the way which all others presuppose, is by being truly Christian precisely where they are, in the place to which their human vocation has called them (*Conversations With Monsignor Escriva de Balaguer*, page 188).

Today, too, the clericalist dialectic supports a kind of *neocongregationalism*[g], expressed in the writings of some theologians and theological popularizers and apparently acted out here and there by people who see themselves as an avant-garde underground Church. (For a survey of theological literature, see Patrick J. Dunn, *Priesthood: A Re-examination of the Roman Catholic Theology of the Presbyterate.* Staten Island, N.Y.: Alba House, 1990, pages 19-44.)

Like many other exaggerations, neocongregationalism starts from an important reality: the common priesthood of the faithful that comes with baptism, as suggested in various places in the New Testament—for example, the first letter of Peter: "you are a chosen race, a royal priesthood, a holy nation, God's own people" (1 Pt 1.9). Long neglected in Catholic thought and practice, this ancient doctrine has come to the fore since Vatican Council II. But at a price—the confusion of neocongregationalism.

So, for instance, an American theologian argues that the "primary division" in the Christian community is not between priest and people but between those who minister within the Church and those who minister outside. "All of these ministries are priestly, stemming from the common priesthood of the faithful....Perhaps we can distinguish between *ministers of the church* and *ministers in the world*" (Paul Lakeland, *The Liberation of the Laity*. New York: Continuum, 2003, page 267).

A Canadian writer goes even further, claiming: "Nothing, absolutely nothing, can be experienced, understood, or done that can be situated *above* or *beside* the baptismal priesthood....[T]here cannot be in history any other Christian priesthood than the baptismal priesthood" (Remi Parent, *A Church of the Baptized: Overcoming the Tension Between the Clergy and the Laity*. Mahwah, N.J.: Paulist Press, 1989, pages 77, 101). The author extends this thinking even to the celebration of the Eucharist, where, he tells us, "certain persons and communities have begun to forsake the schemas of the magical mentality" (Parent, pages 124-125). Apparently this means: celebrate Mass—or what they take to be Mass—without an ordained priest.

Compare this with the teaching of the Second Vatican Council. The Dogmatic Constitution on the Church makes it clear that the baptismal priesthood and the ministerial or hierarchical priesthood "differ from one another in essence and not only in degree" (*Lumen Gentium*, 10). This in fact is a doctrine already definitively taught by the Council of Trent (see Denzinger-Schönmetzer 1771-78).

Although Vatican II does not go into detail about the nature of the difference between ordained and non-ordained, there have been some helpful efforts to clarify it. An important paper published in 1970 by the *International Theological Commission*[g], a body of scholars serving in an advisory capacity to the Vatican's Congregation for the Doctrine of the

Faith, identified the distinctiveness of the ordained priesthood this way:

> [T]he Christian who is called to the priestly ministry receives by his ordination not a merely external function but a new sharing in the priesthood of Christ, by virtue of which he represents Christ at the head of the community and, as it were, facing the community. The ministry is therefore a specific way of exercising the Christian service in the Church. This specific character is seen especially in the priest's role of presiding at the Eucharist, a role that is necessary for the full realization of the Christian worship ("The Priestly Ministry," in Michael Sharkey, ed., *International Theological Commission: Texts and Documents, 1969-1985*. San Francisco: Ignatius Press, 1989, page 87).

The purpose here, however, is not to enter into a full-scale refutation of neocongregationalism, but only to point out that it is one by-product of the clericalist dialectic. Although its exaggerated emphasis on baptismal priesthood is sometimes taken to be a healthy reaction against clericalism, it is in reality a mirror image of clericalist values arising from essentially the same sources: deep-seated confusion on the subject of vocation, pervasive depreciation of the secular order and of the laity's duties there, and an implicit assumption that for lay people to enjoy real dignity in the Church, they must become—and begin to do—what the ordained clergy are and do: in other words, they must be clericalized. We shall have more to say about all of these things later.

In the final analysis, as neocongregationalism sees things, an autonomous baptismal ministry carried on in and to the world by Christians does not count for much. What really matters is the familiar clericalist model of Christian life, with its stress on roles and functions within the safe structures of the ecclesiastical institution.

The shortage of priests and of new priestly vocations in the United States and other Western countries makes it likely that the problems discussed here will persist, and even grow worse, in the years ahead. As long as clericalist ways of thinking persist, we are likely to find that efforts to deal with this problem by multiplying lay ministries—something that arguably should be done for its own sake as well as for the sake of meeting urgent needs for personnel—will heighten confusion concerning lay and clerical identities and roles. We are likely to find more credence given—as a result of this confusion, as well as out of sheer desperation—to the leveling proposal of neocongregationalism. And unless steps are taken to prevent it, we could find the shortage of priests and priestly vocations becoming even worse as these trends reinforce and feed off one another.

These things need not happen. Clericalism increases the chances that they will. And as that suggests, clericalism in all its forms and manifestations has done and goes on doing great harm to all the members of the Church individually, priests as well as laity, and also to the Church as a whole. It is systemic and pervasive. Until it is eradicated, it will continue to injure Catholic life in countless ways.

Searching for Solutions

In seeking solutions to the problems that have clericalism at their root, it is necessary to set aside the idea that the clergy-laity distinction expresses all that needs saying about the fundamental structure of the Church. From a certain point of view, of course, the Church is divided into clerics and lay people, and that represents the will of Christ. Nothing in what follows should be understood in a sense contrary to the explicit statement of Canon 207.1: "By divine institution, among Christ's faithful there are in the Church sacred ministers, who in law are also called clerics; the others are called lay people." But this division of the community of the faithful is not the fundamental fact about it.

More basic than any state of division within the Christian community is its *undivided* state. This can be discerned in the condition of those newly initiated into the community by baptism, who are best described as *christifideles*[g], Christ's faithful people. In ecclesial terms, it is the condition of the Church itself understood as *communio*, a community of persons in communion with God, within which relationships are best understood on the model of the Trinity itself (see Pope John Paul II, Post-Synodal Apostolic Exhortation *Christifideles Laici* on the Vocation and the Mission of the Lay Faithful in the Church and in the World, 18).

This points to a simple but crucially important conclusion: Without succumbing to the confusions and mistakes of neocongregationalist thinking about ministry, it is imperative to give renewed emphasis, in true and appropriate ways, to the radical oneness and equality of all the members of the Church arising from baptism. In our thinking and our practice, we need to balance the Church's very real and necessary division into clergy and laity with the no less real and necessary unity and equality of all the *christifideles*. In fact, considering that the ignoring of this fundamental unity and equality for centuries has done so much to create the debilitating state of mind and corresponding pattern of behavior called clericalism, we need now to give particular emphasis to these central realities of the Church.

The unity and equality of the *christifideles* have dynamic implications. On this basis, it becomes possible for clerics and lay people to discern and live out their proper vocations and apostolates and ministries in ways that are not only harmonious but truly complementary and mutually supportive. It then is clear that the complementarity and interdependence of the Church's lay and clerical members are not merely sociologically convenient but are intrinsic to the very nature and being of the faith community and the *christifideles* themselves. In speaking of such 'community' values, we are not speaking only of what it takes to have pleasant relationships within this particular social setting; we are referring to what is absolutely required to realize the identity of cleric and lay person as they are meant to be.

The International Theological Commission makes this point: "Thus, the people cannot exercise their ministry without [a] priestly minister, but, similarly, the latter—bishop or priest—cannot fulfill his priestly office without the people, for he exists only in the priestly community. 'No Church without bishop and no bishop without Church,' said St. Cyprian" ("The Priestly Ministry," page 52). By contrast, clericalism places exaggerated emphasis upon the clerical hierarchy and very little upon the lay faithful; while the thrust of neocongregationalism, reacting against clericalism, is in the direction of a Church without a ministerial hierarchy.

Implicit in the ecclesiology of the Church as *communio* is an understanding of vocation that sees this one word as standing for three related but distinct realities: 1. the baptismal or common Christian vocation; 2. vocation as state in life (the clerical state, the consecrated life, marriage, the single lay state in the world); and 3. unique personal vocation. So important is vocation in this third sense—unique personal vocation—to understanding where and how lay people fit into the Church's mission, that much of what follows will be devoted to vocation in general and personal vocation in particular.

The clericalist mentality takes it for granted that the clerical state embodies an ideal that in some sense is normative for all members of the Church. Not that clericalists expect everyone to be a priest. But they do suppose that the clerical lifestyle is the standard for measuring and judging the worth of all other Christian lifestyles.

That accounts for a view of the laity widely held in the past and still found today: that to be a lay person is a compromise solution for Catholics who lack what it takes to become priests or religious. Lay people then are judged (and the clericalists among them judge themselves) more or less excellent as Catholics according to how well they mirror the clerical ideal.

No one is personally at fault for the persistence of the strange ideas found in clericalism and its offshoots. These are undesirable elements of a cultural legacy, at least as widespread today among lay people as among clergy and found among 'liberals' and 'conservatives' alike. To a great extent, the remedy for clericalism lies in the fact that lay people, like the other *christifideles*, have true vocations in all three senses mentioned above—the common baptismal vocation, vocation as state in life, and unique personal vocation. To this subject of vocation we shall turn next.

Spiritual Treasure

Anyone who thinks that Christ's voice will not be heard in the world today unless the clergy are present and speak out on every issue has not yet understood the dignity of the divine vocation of each and every member of the Christian faithful.

St. Josemaria Escriva

VI.

Vocations and the Laity

Tearful and absorbed in prayer, Dorothy Day knelt in the shadowy crypt church of Washington, D.C.'s National Shrine of the Immaculate Conception. It was December, 1932, and the *Great Depression*[g] held the nation in its iron grip. Day, a recent convert to Catholicism, had come to the nation's capital as a journalist to cover a hunger march organized partly by communists. She was deeply moved by what she had seen—and distressed to think how little she was doing for the poor and suffering masses to whose service she had felt God calling her for years.

Kneeling in the dim church, she later wrote, "the prayer that I offered up was that some way would be shown me, some way would be opened up for me to work for the poor and the oppressed."

Leaving the shrine, she went to the railroad station and boarded a train for New York. When she entered her apartment she found a surprise waiting for her—"a short, stocky man in his mid-fifties, as ragged and rugged as any of the marchers I had left." It turned out that he was a French peasant named Peter Maurin, an ardent Catholic eager to share his scheme for combining the Gospel and radical social thought in a movement he called the "green revolution." Maurin wanted Dorothy Day to join him in this enterprise.

Neither of them realized it, but the *Catholic Worker*[g] movement had been born.

Most people do not encounter major parts of their personal vocations quite as dramatically as Dorothy Day did. For many, in fact, learning God's special plan for them is a gradual task extending over some years. Indeed, someone reading Dorothy Day's account of her life can see that gradual process in her case, leading up to that sudden flash of insight on a December day in 1932.

But no matter. Whether the definitive comprehension of God's will comes little by little or in a blinding flash (think of St. Paul), the discovery of God's particular plan for them is an experience common to all Christians who sincerely seek to know and do God's will. This is an extremely important point to emphasize and re-emphasize in the case of Catholics, many of whom have been more or less conditioned to believe that they do not have "vocations" in any really important sense.

To understand that point, we need to examine both the general idea of vocation, especially as it applies to the laity, and then the crucial reality of *personal* vocation.

Three Meanings of Vocation

The idea of vocation, especially personal vocation, is of central importance in understanding the role of lay people in the Church's mission. Not only is there such a thing as "the lay vocation" in general—the role that comes with the laity's characteristic situation as people living and working in the secular world—but there also are the unique callings addressed by God to individual Christians: their personal vocations.

But before getting into that, we need to understand the several different, complementary senses that this one word "vocation" has in religious speech. As we saw above, these are: the common Christian vocation which comes from baptism and is reaffirmed and strengthened in the sacrament of confirmation; vocation as a state in life—or, as we might say, a Christian lifestyle or special form of service; and vocation in the sense of unique personal vocation.

It may be helpful to think of these three meanings of vocation on the model of concentric circles, with each successive circle taking for granted and amplifying the previous one. Let us take a closer look at each.

1. The common Christian vocation.

At the center of the circles is the calling common to all Christians. It comes to them from the sacrament of baptism and is strengthened in the sacrament of confirmation. It is the vocation to love and serve God and neighbor and cooperate with God in his redemptive work—the redemption of others as well as themselves.

Lay people share in this vocation along with the other members of the Church, i.e., clerics and persons in *religious life*[g]. The Second Vatican Council says:

> There is, therefore, one chosen People of God: "one Lord, one faith, one baptism" (Eph. 4.5); there is a common dignity of members deriving from their rebirth in Christ, a common grace as sons, a common vocation to perfection, one salvation, one hope and undivided charity (*Lumen Gentium*, 32).

Participating in the life and work of the Church, whose mission is to continue the redemptive work of Christ, is part of the Christian vocation of all.

> Although by Christ's will some are established as teachers, dispensers of the mysteries and pastors for others, there remains, nevertheless, a true

equality between all with regard to the dignity and to the activity which is common to all the faithful in the building up of the Body of Christ (*ibid.*).

Furthermore, all share the "common vocation to perfection"— the universal call to holiness. Vatican II states this important truth in these words: "[A]ll Christians in any state or walk of life are called to the fullness of Christian life and to the perfection of love" (*ibid.*, 39).

2. Vocation as state in life (or Christian lifestyle or vocation to special service).

Radiating out from the starting-point of the common Christian vocation is the first concentric circle of vocation— state in life.

A great deal has been written about the various "states" within the general framework of Church membership and the Christian life, and much of it is difficult to understand and more or less in contradiction to other contributions to this body of literature. But at least it is clear that there really are different states in life that organize the living-out of the common Christian vocation in particular ways.

These states are vocations in a true sense. Vatican II speaks in this way of the priesthood, the *diaconate*[g], the religious life, and the lay state. All four of these are states in life—and vocations. So, for instance, the Dogmatic Constitution on the Church, distinguishing among clerics, religious, and laity within the one People of God, speaks as follows of these different ways of living the Christian life:

> Although those in *Holy Orders*[g] may sometimes be engaged in secular activities or even practice a secular profession, yet by reason of their particular vocation, they are principally and expressly ordained for the sacred ministry. At the same time,

religious give outstanding and striking testimony that the world cannot be transfigured and offered to God without the spirit of the beatitudes. But by reason of their special vocation it belongs to the laity to seek the kingdom of God by engaging in temporal affairs and directing them according to God's will (*Lumen Gentium*, 31).

The states of life are large, more or less clearly defined frameworks within which different individuals carry out the common Christian vocation—to love and serve God and cooperate in the mission of the Church—according to a particular pattern or plan that also is pursued by other people who make the same choice.

The states embody and express in action broad, overarching choices called *commitments*[g]. As commitments, they go very far in shaping the lives of those who opt for them, by reason of the countless implementing choices and actions required over a long period of time by those who make them.

3. Personal vocation.

The final concentric circle of vocation, following upon the common Christian vocation and vocation as state in life, is unique personal vocation. The idea is relatively new, although the reality is not.

The 'stuff' of a personal vocation is the unique combination of commitments, relationships, obligations, opportunities, strengths, and weaknesses that a particular individual who is trying to know, accept, and do God's will uses as the material of his or her living out of the common Christian vocation and a state in life.

As a state in life specifies the common Christian vocation, so unique personal vocation specifies—makes concrete and carries out—the general obligations and opportunities that come with a state in life and the baptismal vocation common to all.

Although it would be an exaggeration to say that personal vocation is a central theme in the teaching of Vatican II, the idea can be found in a number of places. For instance, in the Dogmatic Constitution in the Church: "Strengthened by so many and such great means of salvation, all the faithful, whatever their condition or state—though each in his own way—are called by the Lord to that perfection of sanctity by which the Father himself is perfect" (*Lumen Gentium*, 11). Or this, in a statement on the place occupied by the evangelical counsels (poverty, chastity, and obedience) in the lives of members of religious institutes: "For the counsels, when willingly embraced in accordance with each one's personal vocation, contribute in no small degree to the purification of the heart and to spiritual freedom" (*ibid.*, 46).

Personal Vocation in the Thought of John Paul II

But it is Pope John Paul II who has done more than anyone else to call attention to the reality of personal vocation and make clear its important place in Christian life.

As we have seen, he discusses the vocation and mission of the laity at length in *Christifideles Laici*, "The Lay Members of Christ's Faithful People," his 1989 apostolic exhortation after the 1987 Synod assembly on lay people. Up to now, this is the most important document of the Magisterium on the role of the laity since the great documents of Vatican Council II (1962-65), *Lumen Gentium* (the Dogmatic Constitution on the Church) and *Apostolicam Actuositatem* (the Decree on the Apostolate of Lay People).

Personal vocation is one of the central themes of *Christifideles Laici*—in itself, a notable breakthrough in Catholic thinking and writing about the laity. In an important passage on forming lay people for the apostolic work to which they are called, the Pope writes:

The fundamental objective of the formation of the lay faithful is an ever-clearer discovery of one's vocation and the ever-greater willingness to live so as to fulfill one's mission.

God calls me and sends me forth as a laborer in his vineyard. He calls me and sends me forth to work for the coming of his Kingdom in history. This personal vocation and mission defines the dignity and the responsibility of each member of the lay faithful and makes up the focal point of the whole work of formation, whose purpose is the joyous and grateful recognition of this dignity and the faithful and generous living-out of this responsibility.

In fact, from eternity God has thought of us and has loved us as unique individuals. Every one of us he called by name, as the Good Shepherd "calls his sheep by name" (Jn 10.3). However, only in the unfolding of the history of our lives and its events is the eternal plan of God revealed to each of us. Therefore, it is a gradual process; in a certain sense, one that happens day by day.

To be able to discover the actual will of the Lord in our lives always involves the following: a receptive listening to the Word of God and the Church, fervent and constant prayer, recourse to a wise and loving spiritual guide, and a faithful discernment of the gifts and talents given by God, as well as the diverse social and historic situations in which one lives (*Christifideles Laici*, 58).

Crammed into this passage are a number of extremely important points. Among them are the following.

*The term "vocation" does not refer only to the calling of the clergy and the religious. Rather, the idea and the reality of vocation apply to all members of the Church, including the laity.

*A Christian's personal vocation is not a generic, one-size-fits-all calling shared with others. A *personal* vocation is the unique, unrepeatable role in the carrying-out of his providential plan that God intends each one to play. "Every one of us he called by name," John Paul says.

*Formation[g] leading to the discernment and acceptance of one's personal vocation is fundamental in the formation of lay people. And while there are crucial periods for vocational discernment (typically, adolescence and young adulthood), discerning and accepting a personal vocation should continue throughout one's life. To see and accept God's will here and now is a task for a sincere Christian each day of his or her life.

*Discernment is not a subjective activity, not a form of navel-gazing. It requires attending carefully to the word of God and the teaching of the Church, regular prayer, spiritual direction, and the clear-eyed assessment of one's particular gifts along with the circumstances of one's life. While no one can discern a vocation for someone else, other people do have an important role in the discernment process.

As we saw earlier, the idea of personal vocation has been present to some extent in the Christian tradition for a long time. But its contemporary emergence in Catholic life can without exaggeration be called a revolutionary development, with the potential to change for the better the lives of countless people and the life of the Church.

John Paul II discussed personal vocation not only in *Christifideles Laici* but in many other documents of his pontificate beginning with his first encyclical, *Redemptor*

Hominis, the Redeemer of Man. In this 1979 encyclical, published just five months after becoming pope, he sets out ideas and emphases that would be of central importance in the years that followed. Of personal vocation he writes:

> For the whole of the community of the People of God and for each member of it what is in question is not just a special "social membership"; rather, for each and every one what is essential is a particular "vocation"....[I]n the Church as the community of the People of God under the guidance of the Holy Spirit's working, each member has "his own special gift", as St. Paul teaches [1 Cor 7.7]. Although this "gift" is a personal vocation and a form of participation in the Church's saving work, it also serves others, builds the Church and the fraternal communities in the various spheres of human life on earth (*Redemptor Hominis*, 21).

And here is what he says twenty-four years later in his message for the 2003 World Day of Prayer for Vocations:

> How can one not read in the story of the "servant Jesus" the story of every vocation: the story that the Creator has planned for every human being, the story that inevitably passes through the call to serve and culminates in the discovery of the new name, designed by God for each individual? In these "names," people can grasp their own identity, directing themselves to that self-fulfillment which makes them free and happy (Message for the 40th World Day of Prayer for Vocations, *L'Osservatore Romano*, Weekly Edition in English, February 5, 2003).

Jesus had a personal vocation, expressed by the word "redeemer." The Blessed Virgin, St. Joseph, and the Apostles had personal vocations. So does each follower of Christ today—each has a personal vocation, resembling Jesus' in some ways yet also uniquely his or her own. This is "the new name, designed by God for each individual" of which Pope John Paul speaks.

Karol Wojtyla began thinking about personal vocation long before he became Pope John Paul II. There is an extensive treatment in his book *Love and Responsibility*, first published in Poland in 1960. (See Karol Wojtyla, *Love and Responsibility*. New York: Farrar, Straus, Giroux, 1981, pp. 255-58.)

First of all, he here points out, vocation in any sense is a *personal* reality, in the sense that only persons make commitments of a vocational nature: cats and dogs, we might say, do not and cannot have vocations. The very idea of vocation thus immediately puts us in contact with "a very interesting and profound area of man's interior life"—the area where personal freedom operates.

To be sure, vocations do have an external, social aspect. They come to us from outside, so to speak, and they tend to define the patterns our lives will follow in the world and how we will relate to other people and be of service to them. But they also have the *personalist*[g] significance just noted. "In this other meaning," Wojtyla writes, "the word 'vocation' indicates that *there is a proper course for every person's development to follow*, a specific way in which he commits his whole life to the service of certain values." Furthermore, from the personalist perspective love is of crucial importance. "That a particular person has a particular vocation always...means that his love is fixed on some particular goal. A person who has a vocation must not only love someone but be prepared to give himself or herself for love."

This has more than natural, human significance. It is relevant precisely to vocation considered from the religious point of view, as a crucial factor in one's relationship with God. Wojtyla writes:

> An inner need to determine the main direction of one's development by love encounters an objective call from God.... 'What is my vocation' means 'in what direction should my personality develop, considering what I have in me, what I have to offer, and what others—other people and God—expect of me?'

A person can respond fully and appropriately to the vocational imperative understood in this light only through the "operations of Grace"; he or she faces the need to "learn to integrate himself into the activity of God and respond to his love."

The writer goes on to commend the state of consecrated virginity in glowing terms. But excellent as consecrated virginity is, someone not living in that particular state yet observing the commandment to love God and neighbor can in fact be "closer to perfection" than someone in the state of consecrated virginity. This seeming paradox is unraveled by the dynamic of personal vocation—by the acceptance and living-out of God's particular plan for oneself.

> In the light of the Gospel it is obvious that every man solves the problem of his vocation in practice above all by adopting a conscious personal attitude towards the supreme demand made on us in the commandment to love. This attitude is primarily a function of the person: the condition of the person—whether the person is married, celibate, or even virgin (if virginity is thought of simply as

a status or a factor in the status of the person) is
here of secondary importance.

What comes first is to know and do God's particular will for
oneself; this is the particular form imposed by personal
vocation upon the universal command to love.

Against this background, it is easy to see the origins,
many years earlier, of Pope John Paul II's strong and consistent
teaching about personal vocation and its role in individual
and ecclesial life. The subject is one to which he has repeatedly
returned.

To conclude this brief treatment of the thought of John
Paul II, here is an especially clear statement about personal
vocation found in his 1992 apostolic exhortation on the
priesthood, *Pastores Dabo Vobis*[g]. Speaking of the Church's
duty to form in its members "a desire and a will to follow
Jesus Christ in a total and attractive way," he says:

> This educational work, while addressed to the
> Christian community as such, must also be aimed
> at the individual person: indeed, God with his call
> reaches the heart of each individual, and the Spirit,
> who abides deep within each disciple...gives
> himself to each Christian with different charisms
> and special signs. Each one, therefore, must be
> helped to embrace the gift entrusted to him as a
> completely unique person, and to hear the words
> which the Spirit of God personally addresses to
> him (*Pastores Dabo Vobis*, 40).

Spiritual Treasure

If we love God with our whole hearts, how much heart have we left? If we love with our whole mind and soul and strength, how much mind and soul and strength have we left? We must live this life now. Death changes nothing. If we do not learn to enjoy God now we never will. If we do not learn to praise Him and thank Him and rejoice in Him now, we never will.

Dorothy Day, *The Long Loneliness*

VII.

Personal Vocation

Having been introduced to the idea of personal *vocation*[g], we need to get better acquainted with this very important part of our lives as Christians. Especially, we need to consider the practical relevance that personal vocation has to the lives of Catholic lay people who live, work, and seek to serve God and neighbor out in the secular world.

The so-called vocation shortage is a good place to begin our discussion of these matters.

A Shortage of Vocations—or Something Else?

Is there really a shortage of vocations? Pretty clearly, there is some sort of problem in this area today. That the number of priests and religious available to serve the Catholic community in the United States and some other countries is dwindling becomes more apparent and more troubling as time goes by. But is it correct to call this a vocation shortage? That needs a closer look.

By contrast with the first six decades of the twentieth century, the flow of new candidates for the priesthood and religious life has certainly fallen off in the United States, Canada, and Western Europe. Between 1965 and 2002, the number of priests in the U.S. dropped from 59,000 to 46,000, a decline of 22%, while the number of religious sisters fell from 180,000 to 75,500. More than half of those religious women were 70 or older by the year 2002, while about three out of ten of the priests were retired or otherwise inactive.

The declines obviously reflect deaths and departures from the ranks of clergy and religious. But they also reflect something else: a steep drop in the number of new candidates. Since the number of candidates now falls far below the replacement rate, the number of priests and religious unavoidably will drop further and faster in the years immediately ahead. Efforts to compensate by encouraging aging women and men to stay on the job beyond normal retirement age, seeking replacements from other countries with clergy and religious to spare, and turning to permanent deacons and lay people to plug the gap will help some but won't meet the need.

In this sense, then—a shortfall of new candidates to replace priests and religious who retire, die, or simply quit—there really is a vocation shortage in the United States and some other countries. Already it is causing serious problems for the Church's pastoral ministry, and the problems are likely to get worse.

But granting all that—there is no shortage of vocations. What we are witnessing are the consequences of a shortage of *vocational discernment*[g]. That is a very serious problem, too, but it needs to be understood as what it is, not mistaken for something else.

If many more Catholics—ideally, all—made it a practice to discern, accept, and live out God's particular will for them, the shortfall of new candidates for the priesthood, the *consecrated life*[g], and other forms of Christian witness and service would soon disappear. Far and away the larger number, of course, would find that God was calling them to lives of witness and service as lay people in the world; but many more than now do would find themselves called to be priests and sisters. As the final document of a Vatican-sponsored European vocations congress put it in several years ago: "In the Lord's Church, either we grow together or no one grows" (*New Vocations for a New Europe*, final document of a congress on vocations to the priesthood and religious life held in Rome, May 5-10, 1997).

Other desirable things also would happen. General acceptance of the idea of personal vocation and widespread practice of discernment by Catholics would go a long way toward making an end of clericalist attitudes among clergy and laity and replacing them with a more healthy understanding of clergy-lay relationships. Personal vocation and vocational discernment also are indispensable if lay people are to see and embrace their unique, individual roles in the mission of the Church.

Old attitudes and old ways of thinking currently prevent that from happening. As we saw earlier, one major obstacle concerns the fact that Catholics for a long time have been accustomed to equate 'vocation' with state in life and, in particular, with a calling to the priesthood or religious life. Something the novelist and short story writer Flannery O'Connor (1925-1964) said makes it clear what the consequences of doing that really are.

A correspondent asked O'Connor why it was that she, a Catholic, wrote about Protestants instead of about her fellow Catholics. In reply, she first explained that religion-obsessed Protestants like those whose adventures she recounted "express their belief in diverse kinds of dramatic action which is obvious enough for me to catch." ("I can't write about anything subtle," she modestly explained.) But there was more than that involved.

> To a lot of Protestants I know, monks and nuns are fanatics, none greater. And to a lot of the monks and nuns I know, my Protestant prophets are

fanatics. For my part, I think the only difference between them is that if you are a Catholic and have this intensity of belief you join the convent and are heard from no more; whereas if you are a Protestant and have it, there is no convent for you to join and you go about in the world, getting into all sorts of trouble and drawing the wrath of people who don't believe anything much at all down on your head (letter to Sister Mariella Gable, in *Flannery O'Connor: Collected Works*. New York: The Library of America, page 1183).

O'Connor was making two important points with a bearing on the present discussion. First, that a Catholic who has "intensity of belief" will naturally express it by entering "a convent"—shorthand for: become a sister or a priest. Second (taken for granted by her remarks but not directly stated), that a 'vocation' as Catholics have been taught to understand it is a calling to the clerical or religious state.

O'Connor didn't pursue the point, but the conclusion is obvious just the same. This way of thinking offers little encouragement or incentive to Catholic lay people like herself who are serious about their faith. Rather, practically speaking it consigns the vast majority of Catholics—the laity, that is— to the role of spectators, not players, in the mission of the Church.

And that is a terrible mistake. "Within the Christian community," Pope John Paul says, "each person must discover his or her own personal vocation and respond to it with generosity. Every life is a vocation, and every believer is invited to cooperate in the building up of the Church" (Pope John Paul II, *Message for the Day of Prayer for Vocations 2001*). But telling lay people in effect that they do not have vocations—real God-given callings to active religious commitment and the carrying-out of the divine plan—communicates the opposite message.

Vocational Discernment

Personal vocation is the answer. Essential to grasping, accepting, and living out a personal vocation is vocational discernment.

Earlier we examined Pope John Paul's views on vocational discernment by the laity. His most extensive exposition is in sections 58-63 of *Christifideles Laici*, On the Vocation and the Mission of the Lay Faithful in the Church and in the World. Here are some further thoughts.

Discerning a personal vocation is not the same as planning and organizing a career or even an entire life. Planning and organizing are good and necessary of course, and it is a mistake, a serious fault, not to do these things. But starting there is putting the cart before the horse. Discernment comes first. The planning and organizing should take place *after* one has discerned and accepted God's will. They should be done in the context of the calling one has discerned, to map out the concrete steps one must take to carry out God's will. They cannot take the place of discernment.

This is a mistake that even generous, well-intentioned people sometimes make. Acting in good faith, they attempt to organize their lives as they would organize a project or a trip; the steps in the process include setting goals (get my M.B.A. before I'm twenty-five or my doctorate before I'm thirty), identifying means of achieving them (study at University X or University Y), and then vigorously pursuing them.

Suppose that Bridget, an intelligent and conscientious young woman heading for college, decides that she wants to be a neurologist. She looks around for colleges with excellent pre-med programs, studies hard to get good grades and high SAT scores, and, having consulted her high school guidance counselor, gives careful thought to making her college application essays especially persuasive. Bridget has her eye set firmly and realistically on a worthy goal—an M.D., followed by a career as a successful neurologist—and she is carefully making the right moves to get there.

Good for Bridget! And yet up to this point it has not occurred to her that the most important thing she needs to do—and hasn't done yet—is discern her personal vocation, to learn what *God* wants her to do. If asked about that, she might say, "A career in medicine is a good thing, isn't it? I can't imagine God objecting to *that*." Which is true, of course, but also misses the point.

Typically, people who plan but don't discern organize their lives in light of goals that promise personal satisfaction. Often, they have the support and encouragement of others—parents, teachers, friends—who want them to be happy and share their understanding of happiness as personal satisfaction, as it is measured by a congenial job or career, the esteem of others, a high income—in other words, The Good Life.

Such people aren't necessarily selfish. Their self-set goals may include a substantial amount of service to others. Bridget wants to be a neurologist so that, among other things, she can cure the sick and help them have happy, satisfying lives like hers. And no doubt she is right—God is pleased with that, as far as it goes.

Proceeding in this spirit, people with religious leanings may even turn to some form of ministry, may "join the convent," as Flannery O'Connor put it. Even in these cases, though, the central issue, whether they know it or not, is what will make *them* happy, how they can organize their lives to get the most satisfaction for *themselves*.

The starting-point of vocational discernment is very different: What does *God* want?

That, for example, is the question for two people beginning to think about marrying. *Courship*[g] (the proper name for it, though one not much used these days) is a form of vocational discernment that seeks the answer to the question: Does God mean for us to marry each other?

These days couples contemplating marriage have many questions on their minds: Can we afford it? What about children? Where will we live? Does each of us want to stake his or her happiness on this other party? Often, what God wants gets overlooked. And just from the point of view of the stability and happiness of the prospective marriage, that is a mistake.

As this suggests, vocational discernment is not reserved for a spiritual elite— people who think they may be called to be priests or sisters and nobody else. It should be a regular part of the Christian lives of all members of the Church, something lay people can and should take for granted in living the faith. Catholic schools and parishes need to devote much more time and energy than most do now to encouraging this attitude among students and parishioners, teaching them vocational discernment, and providing them with opportunities to do it.

How to Discern

How do you discern?

Where a large vocational choice is involved—career, state in life, other matters of comparable magnitude—a person discerns by matching his or her circumstances and attributes (strengths and weaknesses, likes and dislikes, existing relationships and obligations, and all the rest) against the needs in the Church and the world and coming to a decision: Do *this* rather than that.

The means of discerning include systematic reflection, earnest prayer, and open-minded consultation with a reliable spiritual adviser and level-headed friends willing to point out things one otherwise might overlook. Retreats and days of recollection can be helpful in providing quiet time for prayer and decision-making. One's choice must be in accord with sound morality and the teaching and discipline of the Church, and, if it involves some form of ecclesial ministry, must be validated by the appropriate Church authority, such as the local bishop or the superior of the religious institute involved. (Far from being extrinsic to the discernment process, these ecclesial criteria are intrinsic elements.)

The discerning proceeds like this.

Spiritual exercises like prayer, receiving the sacraments, and *spiritual reading*[g] naturally give rise to emotions that correspond to one's faith and to elements of one's personal vocation that may already have been interiorized. Carefully reflecting on the options one faces gives rise to another set of emotions regarding them.

The discernment consists in matching the first set of emotions (based on faith) with the second set of emotions (based on the options and reflecting one's inner self). If the emotions of both kinds clearly harmonize better in regard to one option than the other or others, then *that* is the option best suited to one's Christian self and the one which embodies God's call.

It is likely that the right choice will become apparent fairly soon, while the other option or options more or less drop out of the running. We can take it for granted God wants us to know his will. If we make an honest effort to do that, he will tell us what his will is. Peace and confident certainty that in choosing *this* option one is doing what God wants typically accompany successful discerning.

Not every process of discernment needs to be complex and lengthy. Large vocational choices may involve complexity and take considerable time, but smaller decisions about carrying out choices already rightly made often take only a bit of thought and prayer. If Bridget, in our example, discerns that being a neurologist is part of her personal vocation and takes the appropriate steps to become one, discerning where to do her residency, though important, should not take nearly as long as her original choice.

How Personal Vocation Shapes Life

Personal vocation plays a central role in organizing the life of someone who wishes to live according to God's will for him or her. That is because nothing—literally nothing—falls outside the scope of one's personal vocation. People who understand that will strive to make all their decisions in the light of the vocations they have discerned. That, it hardly needs saying, is a lifelong, daily task.

The largest of the choices we make are called commitments. They are crucial to the living-out of our vocations and call for careful discernment before being made. Commitments are overarching choices—something like umbrellas, you might say—that provide a kind of canopy under which many smaller, implementing choices then are made. They shape our identity and indeed our very selves, for they are not so much choices to *do* something as they are choices to *be* something and accept the consequences of that.

Here are a few examples of commitments: the choice of a state in life (priesthood, consecrated life, marriage, the state of the single lay person in the world), which often is mistaken as exhausting the reality of vocation; the choice of a marriage partner; the choice of a major in college that points to a particular profession or career. Commitments like these have a manifestly 'vocational' character. They organize our lives not just in the making of them but because, once made, they call for countless additional choices (along with corresponding behavior) to carry them out, a process frequently stretching years into the future.

Pope John Paul referred to commitments in his 1993 encyclical on moral principles *Veritatis Splendor*[g] when he spoke of "certain choices which 'shape' a person's entire moral life, and which serve as bounds within which other particular everyday choices can be situated and allowed to develop" (*Veritatis Splendor*, The Splendor of Truth, 65). Commitments are the foundation of moral identity. For a Christian, the most fundamental is the commitment of faith, freely made in response to God's gift.

Personal vocation also shapes one's life in a number of other ways. Here we shall consider three: fidelity, hope, and the link between vocation and holiness.

Fidelity to a vocation means being faithful to God's will as it is discerned. That is not always easy to do, and it calls for the best resources of time and talent at our disposal. We need to put everything we have into living our personal vocations. That means no time off—time when we're free to indulge ourselves as *we* want, without reference to God's will. Even seemingly harmless time-killers like vapid TV shows and mindless recreation conflict with the authentic living of a personal vocation, for we should carry out God's will in regard to our recreation as in regard to everything else.

Fidelity to God's call is not immobility. Adaptations and adjustments will often be required in order faithfully to respond to God's will in the shifting circumstances of our lives. But creativity and innovation in living a personal vocation are very different from the compulsive switching from one thing to another of someone who suffers from chronic boredom and a thirst for novelty. Some commitments—the commitment of faith, the commitment of marriage, the commitment a person makes in receiving orders or taking vows—are irrevocable. They must be lived up to and lived out even in the face of disappointment and suffering.

In this world, in fact, even good people honestly attempting to do what God wants cannot escape some disappointment and frustration. Then the temptation to pessimism and cynicism can be strong. "I try to do the right thing—and *this* is what I get," one person says. "No good deed goes unpunished," says another. Christian hope is the answer.

Christian hope is not secular optimism. Counting on human intelligence and will to make everything turn out for the best, secular optimists are peculiarly vulnerable to disappointment and bitterness when—as always happens sooner or later—everything does *not* turn out for the best and people suffer as a result.

But Christian hope looks to the perfect fulfillment of human persons to take place not in this world but the next, and it knows that it will be God's doing rather than ours. Hope like this provides the strength required to live out one's vocation despite the pain that accompanies that. In the light of hope, we can see and accept even disappointment and pain as elements of our vocations—expressions of God's will.

Vatican Council II states the Church's view of these matters in a remarkable passage in *Gaudium et Spes*, the Pastoral Constitution on the Church in the Modern World:

> When we have spread on earth the fruits of our nature and our enterprise—human dignity, brotherly communion, and freedom—according to the command of the Lord and in his Spirit, we will find them once again, cleansed this time from the stain of sin, illuminated and transfigured, when Christ presents to his Father an eternal and universal kingdom "of truth and Life, a kingdom of holiness and grace, a kingdom of justice, love and peace" [Preface for the Feast of Christ the King]. Here on earth the kingdom is mysteriously present; when the Lord comes it will enter into its perfection (*Gaudium et Spes*, Pastoral Constitution on the Church in the Modern World, 39).

In many different ways our personal vocations call us to serve "human dignity, brotherly communion, and freedom" and thus labor to bring about the kingdom of God. Our efforts will have limited success at best. Often they will fail. God's kingdom will not flourish everywhere and always in this world. Still, we persist, believing and hoping that the "fruits of our nature and our enterprise" *will* find perfect fulfillment in the kingdom when the Lord Jesus comes.

Finally, we need to grasp the intimate link between the universal call to holiness (cf. Vatican Council II, *Lumen Gentium*, Dogmatic Constitution on the Church, Chapter V, "The Call To Holiness") and personal vocation.

The call to holiness truly is "universal"—directed to every member of the Church without exception. As the Council says, "all Christians in any state or walk of life are called to the fullness of Christian life and to the perfection of love" (n. 40).

But along with being universal, this call to holiness also is entirely particular—directed to countless unique individuals in the unique circumstances of their unique and unrepeatable lives. Personal vocation is the instrumentality by which God's universal summons to "the perfection of love" is concretely expressed in the lives of holy Christians—past and present, women and men, young and old, priests, religious, and lay people. It is central to the vocation of every follower of Christ to cooperate with him in his redemptive work, but exactly *how* that should be done is, for any individual, a question of personal vocation. And for him or her, it is the way to holiness.

Father Walter Ciszek, S.J., understood that. He tells his story in two powerful books, *With God in Russia* and *He Leadeth Me*.

Trained in Rome to be an underground priest ministering to believers in the *Soviet Union*[g], he entered that country after the outbreak of World War II, was arrested and convicted as a spy, and spent years in prisons and prison camps before being permitted to return home. Subjected to harsh, brutal conditions, he sometimes came to the brink of despair. Then the thought of God's loving providence sustained him.

> God has a special purpose, a special love, a special providence for all those he has created. God cares for each of us individually, watches over us, provides for us. The circumstances of each day of our lives, of every moment of every day, are provided for us by him....
>
> [This] means, for example, that every moment of our life has a purpose, that every action of ours, no matter how dull or routine or trivial it may seem in itself, has a dignity and a worth beyond human understanding. No man's life is insignificant in God's sight, nor are his works insignificant—no matter what the world or his neighbors or family or friends may think of them. Yet what a terrible responsibility is here. For it means that no moment can be wasted, no opportunity missed, since each has a purpose in man's life, each has a purpose in God's plan (*He Leadeth Me*. New York: Doubleday Image Books, 1975, page 231).

That is the heart of personal vocation.

Spiritual Treasure

The creative action of the Christian's life is to prepare his death in Christ. It is a continuous action in which this world's goods are utilized to the fullest. Mary Ann's diminishment [Mary Ann was a young girl badly disfigured by cancer – *editor*] was extreme, but she was equipped by natural intelligence and by a suitable education, not simply to endure it, but to build upon it. She was an extraordinarily rich little girl.

Flannery O'Connor

VIII.

THE LAITY
IN THE MISSION OF THE CHURCH

Start with that word: *mission*[g]. At its root it refers to sending and being sent. When we say someone is "on a mission," we mean he or she has been designated to carry a message or get a job done, usually on behalf of somebody or something else. The word also suggests dedication, commitment of a special sort, as in the case of "missionaries" who are moved by zeal for spreading the faith.

Before ascending to heaven, Jesus sent his followers on a mission: to proclaim the gospel, to announce the Good News to the whole world. St. Mark's gospel says: "And he said to them, 'Go into all the world and preach the gospel to the whole creation'" (Mark 16.15). And St. Matthew: "Go therefore and make disciples of all nations, baptizing them in the name of the Father and of the Son and of the Holy Spirit" (Matthew 28.19).

In speaking of the "world," Jesus meant not just the Greco-Roman Mediterranean culture of those days but the world of all places and periods in history. The mission of preaching the gospel which he entrusted to his first followers was also to be the work of those who would come after them, until the end of time.

That naturally remains true today. "The Church is by its very nature missionary," the Second Vatican Council declared in its Decree on the Church's Missionary Activity (*Ad Gentes*[g], 2). And a little later it spelled out what that means in practice:

> The mission of the Church is carried out by means of that activity through which, in obedience to Christ's command and moved by the grace and love of the Holy Spirit, the Church makes itself fully present to all men and peoples in order to lead them to the faith, freedom and peace of Christ by the example of its life and teaching, by the sacraments and other means of grace (*Ad Gentes*, 5).

This missionary activity takes different forms. It includes preaching and celebrating the sacraments along with programs of social service and human development. In all cases, said Vatican Council II, the ultimate aim of work done in the Church's name is "to open up for all men a free and sure path to full participation in the mystery of Christ" (*ibid.*).

It is not just the Church considered as a collective entity which is on mission—so are all the individual members of the Church. Each one, in his or her own particular way, is called to participate in the mission that Christ entrusted to the Church to carry out on his behalf. It is particularly necessary to emphasize that this applies to Catholic lay people, precisely because the commonly held assumption that they had little or *no* role to speak of was for so long a serious disincentive to their full and active sharing in the Church's mission.

Earlier we saw how the writer Flannery O'Connor summed up this myopic view: "If you are a Catholic and have this intensity of belief you join the convent"—that is, become a religious or a priest. Clerics and religious were responsible for the Church's mission; either lay people had nothing much to do with it, or else their job was limited to prayer and financial support. (The Church's mission does indeed need and deserve the prayers and financial support of the laity. But lay people can and should participate in other ways, too.)

Over time, new thinking on this subject emerged. The laity, it came to be understood, could do work delegated to them by the hierarchy as a form of participation in the hierarchy's own apostolate. As we saw above, this was the Catholic Action model that flourished in the early and middle years of the twentieth century.

Now and then there were exceptions—lay people whose love of God and his Church and force of personality brought them important roles in the Church's mission. One thinks of figures like the nineteenth century American writer and social thinker Orestes Brownson or the great twentieth century British apologist G.K. Chesterton, Dorothy Day of the Catholic Worker movement or Jacques Maritain, the Thomistic philosopher. Many other names of distinguished women and men could be added to the list. Yet such people *were* exceptions. And although thinking has changed greatly in the last several decades, even today the problem of defining the laity's role persists.

Laity and Mission

Now, in fact, some of what gets said about the role and rights of the laity puts the matter in aggressive, adversarial terms. Reflecting the Marxist-tinged thinking of liberation theology, some people suggest that the laity, like members of an oppressed proletariat, should rebel and seize power from the clerical hierarchy. That expresses a ghastly misunderstanding of relationships in the Church and of the Church itself, considered as a hierarchically structured *communio* of persons with fundamentally equal dignity and rights and complementary roles.

But the other extreme—assigning the laity a passive, dependent role—is no less a mistake. If we are to avoid both of these extremes, we need a clear, correct understanding of the basis and source of lay participation in the Church's mission.

Such an understanding is grounded in and arises from the baptismal vocation common to all Christians. The Second Vatican Council's Dogmatic Constitution on the Church pointed to the clear implications of that fact:

> In the Church not everyone marches along the same path, yet all are called to sanctity and have obtained an equal privilege of faith through the justice of God (cf. 2 Pet.1:1). Although by Christ's will some are established as teachers, dispensers of the mysteries and pastors for others, there remains, nevertheless, a true equality between all with regard to the dignity and to the activity which is common to all the faithful in the building up of the Body of Christ (*Lumen Gentium*, 32).

Taking *Lumen Gentium* as its starting-point, Vatican II's Decree on the Apostolate of Lay People supplied additional insights about the responsibility of all members for the Church's mission and the particular forms of participating in this mission to which lay people are called:

> In the Church there is diversity of ministry but unity of mission. To the apostles and their successors [i.e., the bishops] Christ has entrusted the office of teaching, sanctifying and governing in his name and by his power. But the laity are made to share in the priestly, prophetical and kingly office of Christ; they have therefore, in the Church and in the world, their own assignment in the mission of the whole People of God. In the

concrete, their apostolate is exercised when they work at the evangelization and sanctification of men; it is exercised too when they endeavor to have the Gospel spirit permeate and improve the temporal order, going about it in a way that bears clear witness to Christ and helps forward the salvation of men. The characteristic of the lay state being a life led in the midst of the world and of secular affairs, laymen are called by God to make of their apostolate, through the vigor of their Christian spirit, a leaven in the world (*Apostolicam Actuositatem*, 2).

This doctrinally rich passage makes several crucial points.

1. The Church has one fundamental mission carried out by different persons in different ways ("unity of mission" together with "diversity of ministry").

2. As membership in the Church of itself gives the laity a share in Christ's priestly, prophetic and kingly offices, so also it carries with it an intrinsic call to participate in the Church's mission.

3. The special form this takes for lay people is to foster the spiritual well being of persons through the way they live and work in the secular world, infusing the world with gospel values as a kind of "leaven."

Pope Paul VI provided a compelling statement of the laity's role in his apostolic exhortation On Evangelization in the Modern World, *Evangelii Nuntiandi*[g], of December 8, 1975. He wrote:

Their own field of evangelizing activity is the vast and complicated world of politics, society and economics, but also the world of culture, of the sciences and the arts, of international life, of the mass media. It also includes other realities which

are open to evangelization, such as human love,
the family, the education of children and
adolescents, professional work, suffering
(*Evangelii Nuntiandi*, 70).

This is an enormous agenda and a stirring challenge. For, as
Pope Paul pointed out:

> The more Gospel-inspired lay people there are
> engaged in these realities, clearly involved in
> them, competent to promote them and conscious
> that they must exercise to the full their Christian
> powers which are often buried and suffocated, the
> more these realities will be at the service of the
> Kingdom of God and therefore of salvation in
> Jesus Christ, without in any way losing or
> sacrificing their human content but rather pointing
> to a transcendent dimension which is often
> disregarded (*ibid.*).

Consistent with St. Paul's doctrine that the Church is
the Mystical Body of Christ—a body in which the members
have different but complementary roles to play—the specific
ways in which different individuals participate in the Church's
mission are themselves differentiated.

The fundamental form of participation is embodied
in the common Christian vocation. The principles of
differentiation are the states in life (the clerical state,
consecrated life, marriage, the state of the single lay person
in the world) which provide a framework that establishes
general obligations and opportunities for service; and personal
vocation—the unique circumstances of one's life (strengths
and weaknesses, particular obligations and specific
opportunities) in which God's call is discerned. This uniquely
individual and specific call, Newman observed, does not occur
only once or once in a while but instead "takes place now"

and is found in the daily events of life ("Divine Calls," *Parochial and Plain Sermons*. San Francisco: Ignatius Press, 1987, page 1570).

Since in the final analysis no one can discern a vocation for someone else, we can only speak in general terms of how lay people participate in the Church's mission. Individuals must determine the specifics of their callings for themselves (but with the help of others' sound advice, of course).

In general, participation takes three forms: ministry, lay apostolate in the world, and *shared responsibility*[g].

Since lay ministry and lay apostolate have already been discussed earlier, and also because we shall shortly examine several areas of lay apostolate especially commended by Pope John Paul, ministry and apostolate will be mentioned here only briefly and for the sake of completeness. Most of the discussion that follows will focus on the relatively unfamiliar idea of shared responsibility as one appropriate field for lay participation.

Apostolate, Ministry, and Shared Responsibility

The generic name for the mission of the Church is "the apostolate," and so the laity's participation in that mission can be called "lay apostolate." Ordinarily, though, that term is used in a more limited sense—it refers to activity proper and specific to lay people because it takes place in the secular world.

Catholic Action was an important innovation in the understanding of the laity's apostolic role. Its fundamental weakness was the implication that *all* lay apostolate derived from the clerical hierarchy; lay apostolate, according to the Catholic Action model, was a participation of the laity in the apostolate of the hierarchy. As such, it naturally was under the hierarchy's direction and control.

Without repudiating Catholic Action, Vatican II endorsed another version of lay apostolate. The Decree on the Apostolate of Lay People put it like this: "From the fact of their union with Christ the head flows the laymen's right and duty to be apostles. Inserted as they are in the Mystical Body of Christ by baptism and strengthened by the Holy Spirit in confirmation, it is by the Lord himself that they are assigned to the apostolate" (*Apostolicam Actuositatem*, 3). In other words, the apostolate of the laity does not come to them by delegation but by intrinsic right and duty, just because they are baptized and confirmed.

Lay apostolate has a kind of natural priority among the forms of lay participation in the Church's mission. Thus: "The laity...are given this special vocation: to make the Church present and fruitful in those places and circumstances where it is only through them that she can become the salt of the earth" (*Lumen Gentium*, 33). And again: "The characteristic of the lay state being a life led in the midst of the world and of secular affairs, laymen are called to make of their apostolate...a leaven in the world" (*Apostolicam Actuositatem*, 2).

As for lay ministry, it is important to be aware that "ministry" properly applies only to persons who have been ordained. When the non-ordained ("lay ministers") are said to be engaged in ministry, "ministry" is being used in an analogical sense. Since the expression lay ministry is so widely used today, we use it here without further comment, but this crucial point should be kept in mind in order to avoid confusing the ministry of the ordained with the "ministries" of the non-ordained.

Among the key documents on lay ministries is Pope Paul VI's 1972 Apostolic Letter *Ministeria Quaedam*. "Ministries may be committed to lay Christians," it declared. Paul VI spoke specifically of the ministries of lector and acolyte but suggested that other forms of ministry also were possible for lay people.

Ever since, there has been an explosion of writing about lay ministry along with an explosion of lay ministries themselves. This has been a healthy development in many ways, but it also has been accompanied by a great deal of confusion in both theory and practice.

Ever since the 1970s, moreover, the emphasis in official Church circles in the United States and some other countries has been almost exclusively on lay ministry. Organized lay apostolate has suffered a near-total eclipse. This de facto reversal of priorities has been a damaging blow to the Church's mission. It badly needs correcting today.

The third form of lay participation in the mission of the Church is shared responsibility.

Although many present-day Catholics have never heard of it, that was not always the case. In the years immediately after Vatican II there was a great deal of interest in the idea of shared responsibility, which was thought to be an important part of the recent Council's program.

So, for instance, shared responsibility was part of the rationale for the two-conference structure—National Conference of Catholic Bishops (NCCB) *and* United States Catholic Conference (USCC)—adopted by the American bishops in the mid-1960s for their new national *episcopal conference*[g]. As the planners saw it, USCC (whose policy-formulating committees had bishops, clergy, religious, and laity as full members) and a new National Advisory Council (also with a mixed membership of bishops and non-bishops) would evolve into a *National Pastoral Council*[g] for the Church in the United States. The National Pastoral Council would have bishops, clergy, religious, and lay people as members, and would be largely responsible for the Church's social and political action at the national level.

For a number of reasons, that never happened. In fact, events have moved in the opposite direction, *away from* shared responsibility. In 1997 the American bishops voted to abolish the NCCB/USCC structure and replace it with a unitary structure called the United States Conference of Catholic Bishops. Only bishops are members of the USCCB and its committees (but the committees do have non-bishop consultants and staff).

Has the time come to revive the idea of shared responsibility? Some serious Catholics believe it is required by a well-developed theological understanding of the laity and their role—as well as by the practical needs of the Church and the implications of personal vocation. This question should not be reduced to a lay-clergy power struggle, nor should it be seen as part of somebody's program for 'democratizing' the Church. Rather, speaking of the "many benefits for the Church" to be expected from a "familiar relationship" between the laity and pastors, Vatican II's *Lumen Gentium* declared:

> The sense of their own responsibility is strengthened in the laity, their zeal is encouraged, they are more ready to unite their energies to the work of their pastors. The latter, helped by the experience of the laity, are in a position to judge more clear and more appropriately in spiritual as well as in temporal matters. Strengthened by all her members, the Church can thus more effectively fulfill her mission for the life of the world (*Lumen Gentium*, 37).

The Decree on the Apostolate of the Laity declared that "councils" for lay-clergy collaboration on a broad range of issues should be established on the parochial, inter-parochial, diocesan, and inter-diocesan levels "and also on the national and international plane" (*Apostolicam Actuositatem*, 26).

In a report published in 2004, the U.S. bishops' National Review Board, a lay body established by the bishops in 2002 in the wake of the sex abuse scandal to monitor the implementation of the bishops' policy on this matter, offered the following conclusion:

> In sum, the people of God are both clergy and laity. They both have a role. Priests and bishops must learn to trust the laity and not fear their participation in the life of the Church. The lay faithful must learn to exercise their roles within the structures of the Church. The clergy, especially the bishops, teach the faith authoritatively. Lay people do not. The clergy exercise the full power of governance. Lay people do not. But turning to the laity and relying on the participation of the laity does not subvert this structure and does not diminish the authority of the bishops (National Review Board of the United States Conference of Catholic Bishops, "A Report on the Crisis in the Catholic Church in the United States," *Origins*, March 11, 2002, page 682).

This passage points to the important, and difficult, issue of governance in the Church. The power of governance is sometimes said to be linked to Holy Orders in such a way that only those who have been ordained can exercise it. But distinctions are necessary.

Citing the relevant section of canon law (Canon 129), a canonist says lay people "can cooperate...not only in the activity of simple administration, but also in the exercise of power." The nature of the office and its functions are crucial. The writer sums up: "In brief, paragraph one [of Canon 129] states that those *ordained are suitable subjects* or office-holders of the power of governance and paragraph two declares that the *lay faithful can cooperate* in the exercise of this power" (Juan Ignacio Arrieta, *Governance Structures*

Within the Catholic Church. Chicago: Midwest Theological Forum, 2000, page 23).

Pope John Paul II also addresses this question in *Christifideles Laici*. Speaking of diocesan pastoral councils, he says: "The participation of the lay faithful in these Councils can broaden resources in consultation and the principle of collaboration—*and in certain instances also in decision-making*—if applied in a broad and determined manner" (*Christifideles Laici*, 25). He also commends the idea of lay participation in diocesan synods and provincial or plenary councils.

The bishops' National Review Board makes this point:

> Already in the structure of the Church there is a requirement for bishops to rely on the advice, and sometimes even the approval, of consultative bodies such as the diocesan pastoral council or the diocesan finance council. If the laity demand that these bodies truly function—staffed with talented, faithful, independent laypersons giving the bishops honest advice—they are only asking that the bishops follow the law of the Church (National Review Board, "A Report on the Crisis in the Catholic Church in the United States," page 682).

More research into the idea of shared responsibility is needed, along with programs to prepare qualified lay people for this kind of participation.

The Elderly, the Sick, and the Disabled

As a result of baptism and the baptismal vocation, *all* members of the Church are called to participate in the Church's mission. How individuals are to do that is, as we have seen, a question for each one to answer in light of his or her state in life and personal vocation.

The elderly, the sick, and the disabled are called to share in the Church's work along with everyone else. They have important roles in the apostolate, even though these roles may be very different from those of younger, healthier persons.

In his encyclical on human life, having spoken of obligation of families to care for their elderly members, Pope John Paul says:

> But there is more. The elderly are not only to be considered the object of our concern, closeness and service. They themselves have a valuable contribution to make to the Gospel of life. Thanks to the rich treasury of experiences they have acquired through the years, the elderly can and must be sources of wisdom and witnesses of hope and love (*Evangelium Vitae*, 94).

And, in his encyclical on missionary activity, he makes the seemingly surprising point that sick people have a central role to play:

> Among the forms of sharing, first place goes to spiritual cooperation through prayer, sacrifice and the witness of Christian life....I therefore urge those engaged in the pastoral care of the sick to teach them about the efficacy of suffering, and to encourage them to offer their sufferings to God for missionaries. By making such an offering, the sick themselves become missionaries (*Redemptoris Missio*, 78).

And in *Christifideles Laici* he declares:

> The Lord addresses his call to each and every one. Even the sick are sent forth as laborers into the

Lord's vineyard: the weight that wearies the body's members and dissipates the soul's serenity is far from dispensing a person from working in the vineyard. Instead the sick are called to live their human and Christian vocation and to participate in the growth of the Kingdom of God in a new and even more valuable manner (*Christifideles Laici*, 53).

The message is simple and profoundly important: In the mission of the Church there is work for everyone to do.

Spiritual Treasure

The mission of the Church is not only to bring men the message and grace of Christ but also to permeate and improve the whole range of the temporal. The laity, carrying out this mission of the Church, exercise their apostolate therefore in the world as well as in the Church, in the temporal order as well as in the spiritual. These orders are distinct; they are nevertheless so closely linked that God's plan is, in Christ, to take the whole world up again and make of it a new creation, in an initial way here on earth, in full realization at the end of time.

Vatican Council II,
Apostolicam Actuositatem, n. 5

IX.

THE APOSTOLATE OF THE LAITY

At this point some things that have been said here many times need to be said again.

Lay apostolate comes first among the forms of lay participation in the mission of the Church. The Second Vatican Council and Pope John Paul II both make that clear and provide cogent explanations of why it's so. The expression lay apostolate refers to what lay people do in the settings and circumstances of the secular world with the aim of carrying out their duties and performing their roles in the service of God and neighbor.

From this apostolic perspective, the purpose of baptism and confirmation is, as Vatican II remarks, "that they [the laity] may in all their actions offer spiritual sacrifices and bear witness to Christ all the world over....On all Christians...rests the noble obligation of working to bring all men throughout the whole world to hear and accept the divine message of salvation" (Decree on the Apostolate of Lay People, *Apostolicam Actuositatem*, 3).

All this has been said before—repeatedly, in fact. But if it were left at this level of generalization and abstraction, the idea of the lay apostolate would remain a nebulous ideal.

To grasp it as a concrete, living reality, it is essential to get specific.

Yet not *too* specific, not *too* highly detailed. Lay apostolate takes countless forms in countless ways in the lives of committed individuals; any description must remain sufficiently comprehensive to cover them all, open to the creativity and dynamism of Christians who seize opportunities for doing apostolate in novel circumstances and innovative ways. What follows is therefore meant to be suggestive, not exhaustive.

Pope John Paul's apostolic exhortation *Christifideles Laici* offers some guidance on this matter. In sections 36-44 he speaks of eight areas of crucial importance for the lay apostolate in today's world.

These are:

1. promoting the dignity of the person;
2. fostering respect for the right to life;
3. defending freedom of conscience and religious freedom;
4. protecting and encouraging marriage and family life;
5. engaging in works of *charity*[g];
6. participating in public life;
7. placing the individual at the center of socioeconomic life; and
8. the evangelization of culture.

We will cover the first seven here. Because of its special importance and complexity, the evangelization of culture—which in John Paul II's terminology refers especially to media—will be treated separately.

1. Promoting the Dignity of the Person

Appeals to 'rights' are very common today, and the sensitivity to *human rights*[g] is a good and important thing.

Often, though, people claim *their* rights (or what they say are their rights) at the expense of the rights of others.

This happens not just in violent, brutal societies but even in liberal democracies like the United States—societies that pride themselves on being sensitive to human rights. We shall look at some particular examples below. First, though, we need to consider a prior practical question: What can *I* do as an individual to promote the dignity and rights of the human person?

That may be an easy question for political and social activists involved in human rights causes, but most of us aren't activists. What we can contribute to the cause of human dignity and rights is likely to take humble, everyday forms.

For instance: the mother who conscientiously teaches her children to respect the rights and interests of siblings and playmates, carefully correcting them when they violate this norm; the office manager who attempts consistently to deal with subordinates—even those whom he or she finds irritating and troublesome—with fairness and charity; the supermarket checkout clerk who gives every customer, even the annoying ones, a smile, courteous service, and a kind word; the teacher who goes out of his or her way to give students a hand when they are having trouble at home (sickness in the family, an absent father, whatever it may be); the priest who is never brusque with parishioners, not even those who want to talk his ear off or gripe.

None of this may seem profoundly world-changing, yet through these ordinary, everyday displays of respect for other people the world *is* changed into a more genuinely human habitation. "As an individual," Pope John Paul points out, "a person is not a number nor simply a link in a chain, nor even less an impersonal element in some system" (*Christifideles Laici,* 37). Here is a way of promoting human dignity and rights constantly open to everyone in everyday life.

2. Fostering Respect for the Right to Life

The right to life is the basis of other human rights. Declarations in defense of other human rights—"the right to health, to home, to work, to family, to culture"—tend to be "false and illusory," Pope John Paul remarks, if this right is not upheld (*Christifideles Laici*, 38). And that is how things often are in today's world, where what John Paul calls the *Culture of Death*[g] is a powerful force.

In 2003 the Vatican's *Congregation for the Doctrine of the Faith*[g] published an important "doctrinal note" about the duty of Catholic citizens and Catholics in public life to defend and promote ethical values pertaining to the common good of society. Among the specific issues cited were abortion and euthanasia; the protection of the human embryo (e.g., against *cloning*[g], which involves producing embryos in order to obtain stem cells for experimentation, thereby killing them); the defense of heterosexual marriage against no-fault divorce, cohabitation, and the legalization of same-sex marriage; upholding parental rights in education; protecting children against drugs and sexual exploitation; defending religious liberty; fostering economic development; and promoting peace.

In the United States and some other countries, many Catholic legislators and judges support things like legalized abortion and same-sex unions. Under the heading of moral "relativism," the Congregation for the Doctrine of the Faith remarks:

> If Christians must "recognize the legitimacy of differing points of view about the organization of worldly affairs" [footnote reference to Vatican Council II, *Gaudium et Spes*, 75], they are also called to reject, as injurious to democratic life, a conception of pluralism that reflects moral

relativism. Democracy must be based on the true and solid foundation of non-negotiable ethical principles, which are the underpinning of life in society (*Doctrinal Note on Some Questions Regarding the Participation of Catholics in Political Life*, 3).

But the opportunity for lay apostolate extends also to Catholic citizens, who have a serious duty to work for the right to life through their participation in public life, especially by thoughtful, conscientious voting. Unfortunately, not all Catholics do vote in a manner that reflects their duty to uphold and defend the sanctity of human life.

Politics is only one area where Catholic lay people can and should contribute to the defense of human life as part of the lay apostolate. Doctors and nurses have a crucial contribution to make. So do teachers, parents, media professionals, scientists and researchers in new fields of biotechnology, people actively involved in pro-life organizations and groups that assist women with pregnancy-related problems, and persons in many other situations and lines of work.

3. Defending Freedom of Conscience and Religious Freedom

Throughout the twentieth century, and now in the twenty-first, many millions of people have experienced religious persecution, and many have lost their lives. Even today, after the fall of communism, religious liberty is curtailed, and persecution occurs, in countries from the Sudan to China, Saudi Arabia to North Korea. The problem even exists in nations of the 'tolerant' West, though here it takes a different form.

"In many social settings it is easier to be identified as an agnostic than a believer," Pope John Paul II wrote in 2003 in a document on the state of religion in secularized contemporary Europe (Post-Synodal Apostolic Exhortation *Ecclesia in Europa*, 7). To some extent, this phenomenon also exists in the United States, which traditionally has been a highly religious country. Anti-religious bias has existed for a long time in sectors of the American academic and media worlds, and now aggressive secularization efforts are spreading also into health care and social services. The objective is to compel church-sponsored institutions and programs either to conform to secularist views in violation of religious teaching or else go out of business.

Homosexual rights and same-sex marriage are another area of prospective conflict. Under this scenario, a bishop who published a pastoral letter noting that the Church regards homosexual sex as a sin could open himself to charges of hate speech. A priest who refused to officiate at the 'marriage' of a same-sex couple might be accused of violating anti-discrimination laws.

Against this background, the American bishops' general counsel told them at their general meeting in November, 2003: "That government claims the power to remake religious agencies within our society, sweeping aside religious differences, is something all citizens, whether they agree with the Church or not, should find dangerously and deeply offensive....This is not a Catholic issue. What happens today to Catholic social ministries can happen tomorrow to anyone" (Mark E. Chopko, General Counsel, United States Conference of Catholic Bishops, "Protecting Our Ministries in Public Service," November 12, 2003).

Lay people, individually and in organized groups, can and should do a great deal to forestall these developments. Appropriate steps include reaching out to other churches and religious groups to build coalitions, publicly stating their concerns in the media and other forums, and insisting that their elected representatives enact legislative shields against incursions upon freedom of conscience and religious liberty.

4. Protecting and Encouraging Marriage and Family Life

Marriage and the family are under sustained assault today in many parts of the world, including the secularized West. Pope John Paul II, who made defending marriage and family life a central part of his pontificate (e.g., in the 1981 Post-Synodal Apostolic Exhortation *Familiaris Consortio*[g] as well as in a steady stream of other documents and talks), writes:

> The family is the basic cell of society. It is the cradle of life and love, the place in which the individual is born and grows. Therefore a primary concern is reserved for this community, especially in those times when human egoism, the anti-birth campaign, totalitarian politics, situations of poverty, material, cultural and moral misery, threaten to make these very springs of life dry up (*Christifideles Laici*, 40).

As was noted above, the campaign for legal recognition of homosexual "marriages" and "civil unions" marks a new stage in this process. John Paul also expresses particular concern regarding "ideologies and…systems" that seek to usurp the family and parental role in education, and he calls for "a vast, extensive and systematic work" to resist the threats to marriage and family life.

Conscientious married couples are very aware of the secular culture's ongoing assault on marriage and family life—often conducted through the media. Many feel isolated and at risk of being overwhelmed. The agencies of political and economic life often seem to be part of the anti-family campaign, and even religious bodies and institutions offer little help.

In the face of these alarming circumstances, couples and families who wish to maintain traditional values need to come together in groups for mutual reinforcement and support. Where viable family organizations and movements don't exist, concerned couples should take the initiative by organizing gatherings of like-minded married friends, parishioners, and neighbors for social interaction and the discussion of shared concerns. This sort of ongoing grassroots effort to build up marriage and the family in the face of the powerful cultural forces arrayed against them is one of the most important forms of lay apostolate today—one which is at the service of individuals and the whole of society. As John Paul II points out, "the future of humanity passes by way of the family" (*Familiaris Consortio*, 86).

5. Engaging in Works of Charity

The story of the Good Samaritan is one of the most cherished of Jesus' parables. Works of charity performed out of love of God and neighbor have been a central element of Christian life and teaching from the start. "Charity towards one's neighbor, through contemporary forms of the traditional spiritual and corporal works of mercy, represent the most immediate, ordinary and habitual ways that lead to the Christian animation of the temporal order, the specific duty of the lay faithful" (*Christifideles Laici*, 41).

Today, nevertheless, there are real threats to the practice of charity. One of the most serious is the tendency to turn responsibility for works of charity over to the government or organized private charities, or some combination of both, while limiting one's own involvement to paying taxes or making tax-deductible donations.

Not that there is anything wrong in principle with government social services and the large-scale charities of churches and other private groups. On the contrary—they are indispensable. Government and the private sector have serious responsibilities in regard to the poor; well-planned, well-conducted programs of social service and charity by government and the private sector deserve generous citizen support (although occasional abuses—including waste, corruption, and the imposing of immoral policies and practices like coercive population control and abortion on recipients—should be opposed).

But support for organized charities under government and private auspices does not exhaust the obligation of individuals. Pope John Paul makes this point, among other places, in a 1984 document called *Salvifici Doloris*[g]. While warmly commending government social services and the large-scale private charities, he insists on the continued need for "voluntary 'Good Samaritan' work" by individuals and families in hospitals and hospices, homes for the aged, soup kitchens and feeding programs, pregnancy counseling, blood banks, tutoring projects, and other settings.

> Every individual must feel as if called personally to bear witness to love in suffering. The institutions are very important and indispensable; nevertheless, no institution can by itself replace the human heart, human compassion, human initiative, when it is a question of dealing with the sufferings of another. This refers to physical sufferings, but it is even more true when it is a question of the many kinds of moral suffering, and when it is primarily the soul that is suffering (Apostolic Letter *Salvifici Doloris*, 29).

6. Participating in Public Life

Artemus Ward, an American humorist of the nineteenth century, got laughs by boasting, "I am not a politician, and my other habits are good." Joking aside, however, that expresses the casually cynical view of politics and participation in public life which many people now take.

Pope John Paul rejects this attitude. He writes: "Charges of careerism, idolatry of power, egoism, and corruption that are sometimes directed at persons in government...as well as the common opinion that participating in politics is an absolute moral danger, does not in the least justify either skepticism or the absence of Christians from public life" (*Christifideles Laici*, 42). In a democracy people get the political leadership they deserve. If they don't like the results, they usually can blame themselves.

Earlier, in considering the opportunities and obligations for apostolate in relation to the defense of life we spoke about involvement in public life. But that holds true across the board. Upright politics aims to promote the common good in respect to all the fundamental values and needs of the community—it is concerned with the full spectrum of issues relevant at any given time.

The most obvious way to participate in political life— one open to all citizens under the democratic system—is voting. Low voter turnout means many people are shirking their duty. But voting must be conscientious and informed. People often base their voting on frivolous or selfish considerations. But, like holding public office, voting should be based on a sincere and generous calculation of what will serve the common good.

There are many other ways to take part in the political process at the grassroots level: attending and participating in meetings of public bodies, writing thoughtful, well-informed letters to public officials and the media, working for political parties in order to influence them for the better, working for political candidates who meet the criteria of ethics and competence.

Then there is running for and holding office. Catholics in public life are not expected to take orders from the Church, but they have a serious moral obligation to form their consciences and policies in light of the moral truth taught by the Church. The doctrinal note of the Congregation for the Faith mentioned earlier points to St. Thomas More, whom Pope John Paul in 2001 designated patron of statesmen and politicians, as a model who "gave witness by his martyrdom to the inalienable dignity of the human conscience."

7. Placing the Individual at the Center of Socioeconomic Life

During a television discussion the author of a book about corporate responsibility made the following remark: "The basic purpose of a corporation is to make money. No doubt a corporation which treats its employees well, doesn't pollute the environment, and deals fairly with consumers will generally be more successful than one which fails in these matters. Still, the fundamental reason why a corporation exists is to make money, not any or all of these good things."

Probably many people think that way, and to a great extent they're right. Business enterprises exist to make money. In doing that, they contribute to the enrichment of many people besides the owners, including workers and stockholders, while fostering human and social development. Businesses that do *not* make money sooner or later fail, and many people are likely to suffer as a result. If enough businesses fail—as happened in the Great Depression of the 1930s—social stability is weakened and society placed at risk.

All very true. But there is something more to be said. John Paul II, declaring the social teaching of the Church, says it in his 1991 encyclical *Centesimus Annus*:

> The purpose of a business firm is not simply to make a profit, but is to be found in its existence as

a community of persons who in various ways are
endeavoring to satisfy their basic needs, and who
form a particular group at the service of the whole
of society. Profit is a regulator of the life of a
business, but is not the only one; other human and
moral factors must also be considered which, in
the long term, are at least equally important for
the life of a business (*Centesimus Annus*[g], 35).

Although the market economy is an effective
mechanism for generating wealth, the market mentality, left
to its own devices, operates in an impersonal and sometimes
even brutal way without concern for individuals and particular
groups. This can be seen today in practices like downsizing
and outsourcing, where businesses eliminate jobs or shift
operations to regions where labor comes cheap, and in the
unchallenged assumption that certain dead-end, low-paid jobs
are an unavoidable fact of economic life. Efficiency obviously
is essential to the success of a business; it's impossible to
shield all workers from all unpleasant shocks; and not all jobs
can be interesting and richly fulfilling. But businesses and
business managers have a duty to be more sensitive to these
issues than many often are.

Given the complexity of economic life, it would be
foolish to suggest that there are easy answers to problems
like these. But the search for answers should be ongoing, and
many different people and groups should be involved. Boards
of directors, CEOs, executives and managers at all levels,
union leaders and union members, stockholders, consumers,
and public officials—these and others must take on the task
of shaping and sustaining a just socioeconomic order where
human dignity and rights are central values.

These, then, are the first seven areas of lay apostolate
discussed by Pope John Paul II. The eighth area—the
evangelization of culture—is covered separately in what
follows.

Spiritual Treasure

In pursuing its own salvific purpose not only does the Church communicate divine life to men but in a certain sense it casts the reflected light of that divine life over all the earth, notably in the way it heals and elevates the dignity of the human person, in the way it consolidates society, and endows the daily activity of men with a deeper sense and meaning. The Church, then, believes it can contribute much to humanizing the family of man and its history through each of its members and its community as a whole.

Vatican Council II,
Gaudium et Spes, n. 40

X.

THE EVANGELIZATION OF CULTURE: MEDIA

Walker Percy[g], a convert to Catholicism who was a novelist of distinction, once spoke of an "aspect of the matter of the evangelization of culture" that he feared cradle Catholics might overlook.

> It is, or was for me, the very steadfastness of the Church, which is perhaps its most noticeable mark, a steadfastness which is, of course, a scandal and a contradiction to some and a sign to others, as grace permits....By remaining faithful to its original commission, by serving its people with love, especially the poor, the lonely, and the dispossessed, and by not surrendering its doctrinal steadfastness, sometimes the very contradiction of culture by which it serves as a sign, surely the Church serves culture best (Walker Percy, "Culture, the Church, and Evangelization" in Patrick Samway, ed., *Signposts in a StrangeLand*. New York: Farrar, Straus and Giroux, 1991, page 303).

Culture[g] is a pervasive reality. Few forms of lay apostolate are more important than the evangelization of the culture[g]—the attempt to infuse this all-important intellectual, aesthetic, and moral environment with the vision and values of the gospel. The need to evangelize Western secular culture is particularly urgent at a time when it is growing increasingly alienated from its religious roots.

Many persons and groups have roles: parents, by forming their children, teachers and educators at all levels, officials of private foundations and relevant organs of government, leaders in the scientific community, intellectuals and artists, religious and spiritual leaders. The list is very long.

Suggesting the importance attached to this enterprise by the Catholic Church, the Second Vatican Council devoted a chapter of its Pastoral Constitution on the Church in the Modern World to the subject of the Church and culture (Chapter II: "Proper Development of Culture," *Gaudium et Spes*, 53-62).

"The circumstances of life today," the Council remarked, "have undergone such profound changes on the social and cultural level that one is entitled to speak of a new age of human history….The factors which have occasioned it have been the tremendous expansion of the natural and human sciences (including social sciences), the increase of technology, and the advances in developing and organizing media of communication" (Pastoral Constitution on the Church in the Modern World, *Gaudium et Spes*, 54).

In Pope John Paul II's thinking about culture and the need to evangelize it, the communication media occupy an especially important place. In a much-noted passage in his 1990 encyclical on missionary work, *Redemptoris Missio*[g], John Paul likens the communication media to the *Areopagus*[g], the public forum in ancient Athens where people gathered to exchange information and ideas, and where St. Paul famously preached the Good News (cf. Acts 17.22-31). Declaring that the media are "unifying humanity and turning it into what is known as the 'global village,'" he writes:

The means of social communication have become so important as to be for many the chief means of information and education, of guidance and inspiration in their behavior as individuals, families and within society at large. In particular, the younger generation is growing up in a world conditioned by the mass media. To some degree perhaps this Areopagus has been neglected. Generally, preference has been given to other means of preaching the Gospel and of Christian education, while the mass media are left to the initiative of individuals or small groups and enter into pastoral planning only in a secondary way. Involvement in the mass media, however, is not meant merely to strengthen the preaching of the Gospel. There is a deeper reality involved here: since the very evangelization of modern culture depends to a great extent on the influence of the media, it is not enough to use the media simply to spread the Christian message and the Church's authentic teaching. It is also necessary to integrate that message into the "new culture" created by modern communications. This is a complex issue, since the "new culture" originates not just from whatever content is eventually expressed, but from the very fact that there exist new ways of communicating, with new languages, new techniques and a new psychology (Pope John Paul II, *Redemptoris Missio*, On the Permanent Validity of the Church's Missionary Mandate, 37).

And in *Christifideles Laici* Pope John Paul declares media to be "the privileged way…for the creation and transmission of culture" and "a new frontier for the mission of the Church" (n. 44).

Involvement in the media naturally takes many forms, but in all of these it is pre-eminently an area for the activity of lay people. That makes it also a prime area for lay apostolate. To this subject we now turn.

Media and Evangelization

In the last several decades official documents of the Church frequently have exhorted Catholics to make use of the media for evangelization; it would be easy to multiply quotations that make this point.

But this raises a serious question: How realistic is it to think of *using* the media this way? The spectacular success of Mel Gibson's film *The Passion of the Christ*, released in 2004, suggests how much can be achieved when there is a convergence of human and material resources—religious commitment, artistic skill, money. But this seldom is the case. The usual reality in the world of media is something very different.

In their *Pastoral Plan for Church Communication*, issued in 1997, the bishops of the United States put evangelization first on a list of seven activities by the Church in which the media could be of help. But they also acknowledged serious difficulties.

> Church representatives…do not have control over how the secular media portray the Church. Of great interest to many in the media, the Church is, for others, only one voice among many. Some, who are actively hostile, make Church teaching an object of attack or ridicule. Still others see the Church merely as a stereotype of the large institution, to be treated with the skepticism that all such institutions seem to receive in our society. Even Catholic media can project conflicting ideologies which sometimes leave the Church's teaching barely discernible, let alone

communicable. Other limitations include the inherent difficulty of adequately conveying complex Church teaching and policy in a culture that has become accustomed to the sound bite. An equally complex Church structure of overlapping national and local responsibilities can result in a lack of coordination of communication efforts. Finally, financial limitations make it difficult to compete in the expensive world of American media (*Pastoral Plan for Church Communication*. Washington: United States Catholic Conference, 1997, 5).

To this list one might add the handicaps that Church institutions often impose on themselves, including unskilled personnel and excessive, counterproductive secrecy in the conduct of Church affairs (see Russell Shaw, "Lifting the Church's Veil of Secrecy, *Crisis*, January 2001).

Start with the world of broadcasting. (The following account applies specifically to the situation in the United States; making allowances for more or less different conditions elsewhere, however, it also reflects issues and problems that exist in a number of other places.)

One reason why American secular broadcast media provide so few opportunities for evangelization resides in the government's policy decision to deregulate broadcasting starting several decades ago. At one time, local television and radio stations were required to carry public service programming, including religious programs, as a condition for obtaining and retaining their operating licenses; and for that reason the television networks obliged local stations by providing them with a substantial amount of religious programming produced in cooperation with Catholic, Protestant, and Jewish groups.

With *deregulation*[g], however, local stations no longer were required to provide free air time for religious and other public service programs. Now they could sell the time to advertisers—and they did. Thus the stations eliminated religious programming, and the networks stopped producing it. Practically speaking, that was the end of religious programming on network television.

Since then, cable television has arrived on the scene and provided religion with a niche in the cable world. The success of the Eternal Word Television Network illustrates the real possibilities in this area. So, in the world of radio, does the existence of several hundred Protestant-run Christian stations and a much smaller number of Catholic stations. Religion can be found in American TV and radio, but for the most part in a kind of ghetto.

Another serious obstacle—one which Catholics considering communications as a profession need to take seriously—concerns the prevailing attitudes and values in the media.

Media people do not fancy themselves as message-bearers for outside interests. The prickly independence of journalists in particular is legendary. Yet the secular media time and again not only do carry the messages they find ideologically congenial but go out of their way to present them in a favorable light: for example, the messages of secular feminism and gay rights.

Generally speaking, religion is not so favored. That is certainly true with the Catholic Church. A veteran newsman remarked, "As journalists we are under no obligation to give superior weight or credence to an institutional declaration of the Pope or the cardinals or whatever" (Richard Harwood, "The Secular Character of Our Press," in Patrick Riley and Russell Shaw, eds., *Anti-Catholicism in the Media: An Examination of Whether Elite News Organizations Are Biased*

Against the Church. Huntington, Ind.: Our Sunday Visitor, 1993, page 162).

The resistance of secular media to being the Church's partners in evangelization goes deeper than that, however. The question of how the media treat religion is to some extent a question existing within a larger question: How do the media treat most things? A significant change in the tone of journalism occurred in the last several decades—a shift away from healthy skepticism toward unhealthy cynicism. (See, for example, Lee Edwards, *Mediapolitik: How the Mass Media Have Transformed World Politics*. Washington: Catholic University of America Press, 2001.) The same shift appears to have taken place in other countries.

Anti-Catholicism in the Media

The relationship between the Catholic Church and the communication media has special aspects of its own. One of the most important of these lies in the long history of anti-Catholicism in American society. During the 1990s two major studies took a close look at this problem as it relates to the secular media.

The first study was commissioned by the Catholic League for Religious and Civil Rights and the Knights of Columbus, and was carried out by the Center for Media and Public Affairs in Washington, D.C. Using a technique called content analysis, researchers examined four elite news organizations: *The New York Times*, *The Washington Post*, *Time* magazine, and the CBS Television evening news. The analysis examined coverage of the Catholic Church in three five-year time blocks: 1964 through 1968, 1974 through 1978, and 1984 through 1988.

Wanting to know what happened in the decade after the first study, the Catholic League and Our Sunday Visitor commissioned a new study by the Center for Media and Public Affairs covering the 1990s. Along with the original news organizations, the ABC and NBC television evening news programs were added, along with *USA Today*, *U.S. News & World Report*, and *Newsweek*; the study examined news coverage from 1993 through 1998.

The findings of the first study were published in 1993. They did not support the idea that anti-Catholicism was rampant at the news organizations surveyed; the picture was more subtle than that. The executive summary said in part:

> On most controversies involving Church teachings, the Church came out on the losing side of the issue debate reported in the media. Although the opinion breakdown varied from one issue to another, sources supporting the Church were in the minority on the broad range of debates involving sexual morality and Church authority that dominated the coverage. These included heated controversies over birth control, clerical celibacy, the role of women and minorities in the Church, and its response to internal disputes and issues involving freedom of expression ....Controversial issues were frequently presented as conflicts between the Church hierarchy, on the one hand, and lower-level clergy, lay Catholics, and non-Catholics on the other. Journalists frequently approached this subject matter from a secular perspective, structuring their coverage of theological issues along the familiar lines of political reportage.... Ultimately, journalists are less fact-collectors than story-tellers. And the stories they tell about the Catholic Church rely on politics as much as religion for their dramatic appeal. Increasingly, the story revolved around a beleaguered authority struggling to enforce its traditions and decrees on a reluctant constituency (S. Robert Lichter, Daniel Amundson, Linda S. Lichter, "Media Coverage of the Catholic

Church," in Riley and Shaw, eds., *Anti-Catholicism in the Media*, pages 13-14).

The second study's findings were published in 2000. Two stories concerning the Catholic Church had received particular attention from national news organizations during the 1990s: clergy sex abuse and controversy over women's issues. The executive summary said:

> On the whole, national media coverage of the Catholic Church in the 1990s continued to treat it primarily within a framework of political news. This applied both to its external relations to political issues and institutions and its internal authority structures. As it has over the past four decades, the coverage again emphasized the need for the Church to adapt to the more egalitarian and democratic norms and procedures that characterize the secular institutions of American society....As we found in our earlier study, this was not a matter of overtly opinionated or muckraking coverage. It would be more accurate to see it as the reflection of the prism through which one institution — the media — views another with very different norms and traditions (Linda S. Lichter, S. Robert Lichter, and Dan Amundson, "Media Coverage of the Catholic Church 1963-1998," in Robert P. Lockwood, ed., *Anti-Catholicism in American Culture*. Huntington, Ind.: Our Sunday Visitor Publishing Division, 2000, page 220-221).

This is probably an accurate assessment of the general situation. Yet overt hostility to Catholicism, and indeed to religious values generally, does exist in some sectors of the secular media.

It is a frequently documented fact that members of the media elite—the men and women peopling the major news and communication organizations in New York, Los Angeles, and Washington—are much more liberal in their social and political attitudes than other Americans and far less religious. But the problem is larger than that. As a former *New York Times* writer once angrily told a Catholic Church official: "Our secular society has certain needs and imperatives of its own. And it will satisfy those needs and it will act on those imperatives, no matter who objects. And if you and people like you don't like it—that's *your* problem" (quoted in Russell Shaw, "Catholicism: Troubled Relationship Between Church and Media Attributed to a Clash of Values," *Nieman Reports*, summer 1993).

There is a great need for committed lay Catholics and other religious believers to enter the field of secular communications and, in a manner entirely consistent with their professional responsibilities, seek to influence the media for the better. But no one contemplating this work as a possible career should ignore the very real obstacles existing there. Thorough preparation—including not just professional training but spiritual and religious formation—is an essential prerequisite.

As for the use of media for evangelization, several conclusions suggest themselves.

First, in the United States and countries like, it is usually unrealistic to think of *using* the secular media for the direct evangelization of culture. The success of a project like *The Passion of the Christ* simply underlines the general rule: such achievements are rare and very difficult to repeat. For the most part, secular media are not available to be used for evangelization or to be evangelized themselves. Often they are obstacles to evangelization, not vehicles for accomplishing it.

Second, where media and evangelization are concerned, the Church must rely on its own media—Catholic books, the Catholic press, church-sponsored radio and television and audiovisuals, etc. But Church media also have severe limitations, including the fact that they are divided—conservative vs. liberal, traditional vs. progressive, right vs. left—and the fact that, with few exceptions, they reach only Catholics who are already convinced and committed. The role of Catholic media mainly is to motivate and educate the potential evangelizers rather than to communicate directly with those most in need of being evangelized.

Third, the exception to all this is the Internet, where many of the limitations present in traditional media do not exist. Obviously, the Internet has serious faults and weaknesses of its own, including the presence of pornography and commercialism. But where evangelization is concerned, its greatest weakness may also be its greatest strength—namely, the opportunity it offers for direct, immediate, unfiltered, uncensored communication of a message (in this case, the message of the gospel). As the Holy See has pointed out:

> Although the virtual reality of cyberspace cannot substitute for real interpersonal community, the incarnational reality of the sacraments and the liturgy, or the immediate and direct proclamation of the gospel, it can complement them, attract people to a fuller experience of the life of faith, and enrich the religious lives of users (Pontifical Council for Social Communications, *The Church and Internet*, 2002, 5).

Responsible Use of the Media

There is another dimension to the question of media and evangelization which deserves mention here: it is the responsible *use* media by individual readers and listeners and viewers, and also the training of children and young people in responsible media use imparted by parents and others responsible for their formation.

Professional communicators are not the only ones with ethical responsibilities, says the Pontifical Council for Social Communications. The audiences of media have responsibilities, too; and "communicators attempting to meet their responsibilities deserve audiences conscientious about theirs" (*Ethics in Communications*, 2000, 25).

> The first duty of recipients of social communication is to be discerning and selective. They should inform themselves about media— their structures, mode of operation, contents—and make responsible choices, according to ethically sound criteria, about what to read or watch or listen to. Today everybody needs some form of continuing media education, whether by personal study or participation in an organized program or both (*ibid.*).

The Vatican agency goes on to speak of the role of Catholic schools and, especially, of Catholic parents in the *media education*[g] of children and youth. So does Pope John Paul II in several of his statements for the Church's annual World Communications Day. In 2004, in a statement entitled *The Media and the Family: A Risk and a Richness*, he wrote:

> Parents, as the primary and most important educators of their children, are also the first to teach them about the media. They are called to train their offspring in the "moderate, critical, watchful and prudent use of the media" in the home (*Familiaris Consortio*, 76). When parents do that consistently and well, family life is greatly enriched. Even very young children can be taught important lessons about the media: that they are

produced by people anxious to communicate messages; that these are often messages to do something — to buy a product, to engage in dubious behavior — that is not in the child's best interests or in accord with moral truth; that children should not uncritically accept or imitate what they find in the media. Parents also need to regulate the use of media in the home. This would include planning and scheduling media use, strictly limiting the time children devote to media, making entertainment a family experience, putting some media entirely off limits and periodically excluding all of them for the sake of other family activities. Above all, parents should give good example to children by their own thoughtful and selective use of media. Often they will find it helpful to join with other families to study and discuss the problems and opportunities presented by the use of media. Families should be outspoken in telling producers, advertisers, and public authorities what they like and dislike (Pope John Paul II, *The Media and the Family: A Risk and a Richness*, Message for the 38th World Communications Day, 2004, 5).

For Catholic lay people for whom the evangelization of culture is part of their participation in the mission of the Church, this form of evangelization offers enormous opportunities and challenges. As Pope John Paul's words suggest, however, the evangelization of culture, like so many other things, begins at home.

Spiritual Treasure

The opportunities for evangelization arise, paradoxically enough, from those very cultural traits which seem to oppose the evangel—the secularism, if you will, of modern societies, especially American—the consumerism, the scientism, the so-called secular humanism. No, not precisely from the secularization itself, but from its having run its course, from its exhaustion. To paraphrase David Riesman and Jose Ortega y Gasset, there is no lonelier crowd than the mass man, the anonymous consumer who has exhausted the roster of "need satisfactions," as the expression goes, whether the latter be the consumption of the manifold goods of a sophisticated consumer society or the services of the four hundred or so different schools of psychotherapy.

Walker Percy

XI.

THE SPIRITUALITY OF THE LAITY

Ask someone what the obstacles to Christian perfection are, and the answer is likely to be, "The world, the flesh, and the devil." The world comes first.

This negativism about "the world" points to a serious problem for lay *spirituality*[g]. For the world — shorthand for a complex network of structures, institutions, and relationships (family, work, friendships, educational and cultural influences, systems of governance and economic life, etc.) — is the environment in which lay people are obliged to live and work out their salvation.

That means the world, for good or ill, will powerfully affect the quest for Christian perfection by the laity. If lay people are to become saints, they must become saints in the world. Recognizing that fundamental fact, the Second Vatican Council calls upon the laity not to "separate their union with Christ from their ordinary life; but through the very performance of their tasks, which are God's will for them, actually promote the growth of their union with him" (Decree on the Apostolate of Lay People, *Apostolicam Actuositatem*, 4).

We need to reflect seriously on these things.

The Problem of 'The World'

Many years ago, a young Catholic layman was invited to speak on lay spirituality at a Catholic seminary. He took a line not untypical of that day: The spiritual life of the laity was a difficult and hazardous enterprise; and the biggest problem of all was precisely this thing called "the world" where lay people unfortunately had to live.

From a spiritual perspective, he went on, the world was mainly a source of temptations and distractions. The best thing a lay person serious about the pursuit of sanctity could do was withdraw from the world as much as possible and work on cultivating a spiritual life that, as much as circumstances allowed, resembled the spirituality of monks and nuns. That lay people might actually *use* the world as material for their spiritual lives simply didn't occur to the young man, despite the fact that countless lay people had been doing that for a very long time, whether they or anyone else recognized it.

The young man was not alone in missing the point. Back then, most other people missed it, too. The point of view he expressed reflected the attitude toward the world and the laity's awkward situation in it that had characterized much of the thinking about lay people and their spiritual lives for centuries. This attitude was summed up in the expression *contemptus mundi*[g], "contempt of the world." It pervaded a great deal of spiritual writing, notably including that classic work *The Imitation of Christ*[g]—for example, this passage from its opening section:

> It is therefore a great vanity to labor inordinately for worldly riches that will shortly perish or to covet honor or any other inordinate pleasures or fleshly delights in this life, for which a man after this life will be sorely and grievously punished. How great a vanity it also is to desire a long life

and to care little for a good life; to heed things of the present and not to provide for things that are to come; to love things that will shortly pass away and not to haste where joy is everlasting....Study, therefore, to withdraw the love of your soul from all things that are visible, and to turn it to things that are invisible (Thomas à Kempis, *The Imitation of Christ*, Book I,1. New York: Doubleday Image Books, 1955).

There is a great deal of Christian wisdom in that of course, and it is this wisdom which makes *The Imitation of Christ* the enduring spiritual classic it is. But the frequent repetition of this view of the world and its place in the spiritual life—matters treated in one-sidedly negative terms—skewed the picture of the secular environment inhabited by the laity and raised needless obstacles to achieving holiness there. For instance, it reinforced the clericalist mentality, shared by many laity and clergy, which held that in matters of the spirit, the lay state itself virtually guaranteed mediocrity.

Evidently there was need for a new way of thinking—about the laity and also about the world. And eventually this new thinking began to emerge. It can be found in precursors of Vatican II like St. Josemaria Escriva, the founder of Opus Dei. In a noteworthy homily which he preached in 1967, soon after the Council, he declared:

No! We cannot lead a double life. We cannot be like schizophrenics, if we want to be Christians. There is just one life, made of flesh and spirit. And it is this life which has to become, in both soul and body, holy and filled with God. We discover the invisible God in the most visible and material things. There is no other way. Either we learn to find our Lord in ordinary, everyday life, or else we shall never find him ("Passionately

Loving the World," October 8, 1967, in *Conversations With Monsignor Escriva de Balaguer*. Manila: Sinag-Tala Publishers, 1977, page 193).

This was a far cry from the *contemptus mundi* of former times.

Vatican II and Lay Spirituality

In taking up the question of the laity and their spirituality, then, the fundamental issue faced by Vatican Council II concerned the world and the value of human life there. The long tradition of *contemptus mundi* had in fact assigned it very little value. The story is told of a desert hermit in the early Christian centuries who spent the time he didn't give to prayer and mortification weaving baskets; when he had woven enough of them, he piled them high and burned them.

It was a strikingly symbolic way to express the thought that human life was fleeting, the world soon would pass away, and all that really mattered was life in heaven—eternal life. Life here and now was only a kind of test: If you passed the test (lived decently in line with the moral law and the law of the Church), you would get eternal life as a reward; if you failed—lived badly, that is—you would spend eternity in hell. The emphasis was on discontinuity, disconnectedness, between this world and the world to come; such connectedness as there was resembled the connection between passing a test and getting a reward (or failing and being punished).

Vatican II took a profoundly different view. It is found in nn. 38-39 of the Pastoral Constitution in the Church in the Modern World, *Gaudium et Spes*, in a section called "Human Activity: Its Fulfillment in the Paschal Mystery." Up to now it has gotten far less attention than it deserves, possibly because its implications are so remarkable that they still haven't sunk in.

The passage says that in the Incarnation, the Word of God entered human history—entered the world. In doing so, Christ revealed that "the fundamental law of human perfection, and consequently of the transformation of the world, is the new commandment of love." He offered assurance to those who would take this message to heart that their efforts to establish a fellowship of love among human beings would not be in vain.

The love in question is not for special occasions only. It should be brought to bear upon "the ordinary circumstances of daily life." Christ is at work here and now, not only inspiring people to desire eternal life but encouraging them to "make life more humane and conquer the earth" for its sake. Some are called to testify to the life to come, others to dedicate themselves to serving their fellows here and now and in this manner "to prepare the way for the kingdom of heaven." In the Eucharist, where "natural elements, the fruits of man's cultivation, are changed into His glorified Body and Blood," Christ has left us a foretaste of that.

We do not know when or how the world and human beings will be transformed and fulfilled, but we do know this world, marred by sin, is passing away, while God prepares "a new earth" for his children. Citing scriptural passages that speak of the world to come, the Council says that in that new and better life "charity and its works will remain and all of creation...will be set free from its bondage to decay."

Yes, Scripture does teach that it would be useless to gain the whole world and suffer the loss of one's soul. But true as that is, "far from diminishing our concern to develop this earth, the expectancy of a new earth should spur us on, for it is here that the body of a new human family grows, foreshadowing in some way the age which is to come." Earthly progress must be distinguished from the spread of Christ's kingdom, yet it is vitally important to the kingdom of God, for it can contribute to the better ordering of human society.

Precisely from the point of view of the eschatological vision presented in *Gaudium et Spes*, though, there is another, more profound explanation of the importance of earthly progress and human activity to bring it about. Vatican II states it in the climactic statement of this remarkable passage, which was quoted earlier but deserves to be quoted again:

> When we have spread on earth the fruits of our nature and our enterprise—human dignity, brotherly communion, and freedom—according to the command of the Lord and in his Spirit, we will find them once again, cleansed this time from the stain of sin, illuminated and transfigured, when Christ presents to his Father an eternal and universal kingdom "of truth and life, a kingdom of holiness and grace, a kingdom of justice, love and peace" [Preface for the Feast of Christ the King]. Here on earth the kingdom is mysteriously present; when the Lord comes it will enter into its perfection (*Gaudium et Spes*, 39).

It would be presumptuous to claim fully to understand what this means. But at least the teaching of the Second Vatican Council makes this clear: Considered in the light of eternity, the results of human activity in this world are not merely transitory; the continuity between this life and the next is vastly more important than the discontinuity, and this continuity is an intrinsic one that far exceeds the relationship of a test to the reward or punishment that comes with passing or failing. Our good deeds done here and now help build up the kingdom of God; perfected and brought to fulfillment, in ways we cannot now hope to grasp, they last for eternity.

The Council speaks of a universal call to holiness which extends to the laity just as it does to the other members of the Church and, embracing all worthy elements of the lay life in the world, makes of them the elements of our sanctification. *"The Call to Holiness[g]"* is the title of Chapter V of the Dogmatic Constitution on the Church, *Lumen Gentium* (39-42). Its central statement, one that sweeps away centuries of relegating lay persons to a second-tier, minimalistic spirituality, is this:

> It is therefore quite clear that all Christians in any state or walk of life are called to the fullness of Christian life and to the perfection of love, and by this holiness a more human manner of life is fostered also in earthly society. In order to reach this perfection the faithful should use the strength dealt out to them by Christ's gift, so that, following in his footsteps and conformed to his image, doing the will of God in everything, they may wholeheartedly devote themselves to the glory of God and to the service of their neighbor (*Lumen Gentium*, 40).

Lest there be any doubt, the Council Fathers at once add that "although the forms and tasks of life are many," nevertheless "holiness is one."

And what is holiness? Precisely this: "…that sanctity which is cultivated by all who act under God's Spirit and, obeying the Father's voice and adoring God the Father in spirit and in truth, follow Christ, poor, humble and cross-bearing, that they may deserve to be partakers of his glory" (*Lumen Gentium*, 41). Thomas à Kempis was emphatically right about the essential point: For a Christian, holiness *is* the imitation of Christ.

At the same time, of course, the path of holiness is found in someone's particular gifts and duties. Vatican II speaks of Christian married couples and parents, of widows and single people, of workers, the poor, the infirm, and the sick. "All Christians, in the conditions, duties and circumstances of their life and through all these, will sanctify themselves more and more if they receive all things with faith from the hand of the heavenly Father and cooperate with the divine will" (*Lumen Gentium*, 41). The Council does not use the term "personal vocation" here, yet it expresses the heart of the idea while underlining the link between one's personal vocation and one's sanctification.

Vatican II does not lay out a full program of lay spirituality, but it does highlight its most important elements: the practice of charity "by which we love God above all things and our neighbor because of him;" frequent reception of the sacraments, especially the Eucharist, and participation in the liturgy (*ibid.*); "prayer, self-denial, active brotherly service and the practice of all virtues." Like clerics and those in consecrated life, lay women and men are "invited and obliged to holiness and the perfection of their own state of life" (n. 42).

A Genuinely *Lay* Spirituality

As we have seen, Pope John Paul identifies ongoing vocational discernment as the fundamental purpose of the formation of the laity and spells out what it involves: "...a receptive listening to the Word of God and the Church, fervent and constant prayer, recourse to a wise and loving spiritual guide, and a faithful discernment of the gifts and talents given by God, as well as the diverse social and historic situations in which one lives" (*Christifideles Laici*, 58).

In order to live out a personal vocation as the path to holiness, a person needs a plan of life—a combination of road map and schedule, if you will, that spells out in some detail the elements of a serious, well-integrated spirituality.

For Catholics, these naturally will include frequent participation in the liturgy and reception of the sacraments, especially the Eucharist and Penance; regular mental prayer and devotional practices; the practice of mortification in order to strengthen the will and bring the passions under control; examination of conscience; and daily reading of the New Testament and some other sound spiritual reading (e.g., books like *The Introduction To the Devout Life*[g] by St. Francis de Sales, the autobiographies of St. Teresa of Avila and St. Thérèse of Lisieux, the homilies of John Henry Newman and St. Josemaria Escriva, and other reliable classics); and an annual retreat.

Apostolate, either alone or in company with others, should be part of the plan, as should continuing efforts to infuse one's milieu—workplace, classroom, home, neighborhood—with gospel values. Spiritual direction from a trustworthy advisor is essential both for beginners and those who are more advanced. These and other elements of a sound "plan" are discussed in books like *This Tremendous Lover* by Eugene Boylan and other solid guides that reflect the Catholic tradition.

The form of spirituality sought and practiced by a lay person should be genuinely *lay*—suited to and incorporating the circumstances of persons who live in the world, have families and secular jobs, pursue the same interests and engage in essentially the same activities as their friends and colleagues. Although it is certainly true that, as Vatican II observes, "holiness is one," different spiritualities suit different ways of life, and it is a mistake to try to force lay people living in the world to adopt a spirituality suited to religious. For example: although there is no reason why a lay person shouldn't use parts of the Liturgy of the Hours for personal prayer, either regularly or now and then, it would be folly for him or her to imitate cloistered religious by chanting the "hours" around the clock.

Unity of life is imperative. "One of the gravest errors of our time," says Vatican II, "is the dichotomy between the faith which many profess and the practice of their daily lives" (*Gaudium et Spes*, 43). Negatively, avoiding that error means *not* keeping one's spiritual life and everyday secular life in separate compartments, *not* limiting "religion" to a single day of the week, but, in an altogether natural way, living the life of faith and the life of family, work, recreation, and so on as one single, integrated life.

The formation of the laity, Pope John Paul says, must take fully into account "the union which exists from their being members of the Church and citizens of human society."

> There cannot be two parallel lives in their existence: on the one hand, the so-called "spiritual" life, with its values and demands; and on the other, the so-called "secular" life, that is, life in a family, at work, in social relationships, in the responsibilities of public life and in culture....Every activity, every situation, every precise responsibility—as, for example, skill and solidarity in work, love and dedication in the family and the education of children, service to society and public life and the promotion of truth in the area of culture—are the occasions ordained by Providence for a "continuous exercise of faith, hope and charity [footnote reference *Apostolicam Actuositatem*, 4]" (*Christifideles Laici*, 59).

As this suggests, family life and work call for special emphasis in developing and attempting to practice an authentically lay spirituality. Unfortunately, under the influence of an excessive, one-sided notion of *contemptus mundi*, much traditional spiritual writing has had difficulty seeing these as useful elements in the effort to practice love of God and neighbor and achieve "the fullness of Christian life."

Instead, there has been a tendency to view marriage and family as concessions to human weakness and distractions from the interior life making spiritual mediocrity all but certain. (As we saw earlier, realizing that he was called to marriage rather than the monastic life provoked a personal crisis for Thomas More.) Work often was considered to be punishment for original sin as well as a source of temptations to commit new, personal sins. Not much encouragement in that for lay people who might wish to cultivate unity of life.

Modern times have witnessed a great change in this way of thinking. Marriage, family life, and work now are understood as, potentially at least, fruitful elements in the spiritual lives of lay people. This is not the place to set out a fully developed theology and spirituality of either work or of marriage. But it is worth mentioning a few key points made by Pope John Paul.

The fullest exposition of his thinking on marriage and family is found in *Familiaris Consortio*, an apostolic exhortation published in 1981 in response to the world Synod of Bishops on the family that was held the previous year. Its exalted view of marriage and family life, and their potential for sanctifying married couples and family members, are suggested in a passage like this: "But in the Lord Christ, God takes up this human need, confirms it, purifies it and elevates it, leading it to perfection through the Sacrament of Matrimony: the Holy Spirit, who is poured out in the sacramental celebration, offers Christian couples the gift of a new communion of love that is the living and real image of that unique unity which makes of the Church the indivisible Mystical Body of the Lord Jesus" (Apostolic Exhortation *Familiaris Consortio*, 19). Marriage and family are a privileged path to sanctity for those who approach them in this spirit.

John Paul II's principal treatment of work is found in the encyclical *Laborem Exercens*[g], published in 1981. In a discussion of "Elements for a Spirituality of Work" in its fifth section, he points to two principal Christian meanings of this universal human activity: Work means co-creation and co-redemption.

Regarding the co-creative dimension, he speaks of the "fundamental truth" that the human person, created in God's image, "shares by his work in the activity of the Creator" and, within the limits of human capability, "in a sense continues to develop that activity, and perfects it as he advances further and further in the discovery of the resources and values contained in the whole of creation" (encyclical *Laborem Exercens*, 25).

As for work's co-redemptive character, John Paul says:

> All work, whether manual or intellectual, is inevitably linked with toil....[This presents] the Christian and everyone who is called follow Christ with the possibility of sharing lovingly in the work Christ came to do. This work of salvation came about through suffering and death on a Cross. By enduring the toil of work in union with Christ crucified for us, man in a way collaborates with the Son of God for the redemption of humanity. He shows himself a true disciple of Christ by carrying the cross in his turn every day in the activity that he is called upon to perform (encyclical *Laborem Exercens*, 27).

There is rich material for prayerful reflection and much opportunity for spiritual growth in the work of lay people who approach their work in this way. The call to the laity to achieve the perfection of charity in and through their lives in the secular world truly is a call to sanctity of a high order.

Spiritual Treasure

Christ has no body now on earth but yours; no hands but yours; no feet but yours. Yours are the eyes through which the compassion of Christ must look out on the world. Yours are the feet with which He is to go about doing good. Yours are the hands with which He is to bless His people.

St. Teresa of Avila

XII.

CURRENT CHALLENGES FOR THE LAITY

The world is a fundamentally good place—for Catholic lay people, the place where they are called to work out their salvation and strive for holiness, which includes promoting human progress and working for justice and peace. At the same time, a truthful picture of the world must include the fact that, alongside the good, the secular order presents large problems and obstacles for serious Christians who wish to live by and proclaim the gospel's message.

The philosopher Josef Pieper sums up the situation like this:

> The "world" exists not only as God's creation. There is also the "world" which, as St. John the Apostle says, "lies in evil" and prevails in the "gratification of corrupt nature, gratification of the eyes, and the empty pomp of living" [another translation: "lust of the flesh, lust of the eyes, and pride of life"] (I John 22, 16); there is the kingdom of the "Prince of this world" (John 12, 31, Luke 4,6); there is the world for which Christ the Lord did not want to pray (John 17,9). There is not only the reality of creation, but also the perversion of the order of creation, which has taken on form in

> the activities of men and the objective "creations" which grow out of these (Josef Pieper, *The Four Cardinal Virtues*. New York: Harcourt, Brace & World, 1965, page 172).

In other words, there is the world as it has been marred by sin—a world that now provides the setting for, and in some ways the inducement to, the committing of further sins. This, too, is part of the reality of "the world."

Most serious-minded and honest religious believers do not need to be persuaded of these things. They are all too familiar with the fact of personal sin—in themselves and in the world around them. As for *original sin*[g], they would agree with John Henry Newman's account of it in his autobiographical masterpiece, the *Apologia Pro Vita Sua*:

> And so I argue about the world—if there be a God, since there is a God, the human race is implicated in some terrible aboriginal calamity. It is out of joint with the purposes of its Creator. This is a fact, a fact as true as the fact of its existence; and thus the doctrine of what is theologically called Original Sin becomes to me almost as certain as that the world exists (John Henry Cardinal Newman, *Apologia Pro Vita Sua*. New York: Longmans, Green and Co., 1947, page 220).

Christian writers from the start have warned against the sinfulness abundantly present in human hearts and in the world.

In this context, it is easy to understand the distress felt by the influential Thomistic philosopher *Jacques Maritain*[g] regarding an attitude he found to be increasingly common among Catholics in the 1960s. As we saw earlier, he called it "kneeling before the world."

What then do we see around us? In large sectors of both clergy and laity (but it is the clergy who set the example), hardly is the word "world" pronounced when a gleam of ecstasy lights up the face of one and all....Anything that would risk calling to mind the idea of asceticism, mortification, or penance is automatically shelved as a matter of course....In other words, there is henceforth only the earth. A complete *temporalization of Christianity!* (Jacques Maritain, *The Peasant of the Garonne.* New York: Macmillan Paperbacks, 1969, pages 68-69, 71; emphasis in original)

It was all the more noteworthy that the indictment of this peculiar "kneeling" should be delivered by Maritain, an ardent exponent of Christian humanism who exercised a profound intellectual influence upon the Second Vatican Council and its program of Christian engagement with the world. Long before the Council ended, nevertheless, he was greatly troubled by the growing tendency among his co-religionists to ignore the fact that the world, in one dimension of its reality, was—and always had been and always would be—nothing less than "the adversary of the saints."

What 'Kneeling' Looks Like

What comes from ignoring, and in practice denying, this fundamental fact about the world can now be seen in the troubles afflicting the Church in the United States and a number of other Western countries. The assimilation of Catholics and other Christians into the essentially hostile secular culture has had disastrous consequences for faith.

Of course there are many explanations for what has happened; but the error of kneeling before the world, rather than seeking to convert it to the gospel, ranks high on the list. Thus, in large sectors of the Western world today, one encounters the phenomenon described by Pope John Paul II: "It is easier to be identified as an agnostic than a believer" (Post Synodal Apostolic Exhortation *Ecclesia in Europa*, 7).

Pope John Paul was speaking specifically of Europe, but the situation of Catholicism in the United States is not a great deal better. For example:

Between 1965 and 2002, the number of priests in the U.S. dropped from 59,000 to 46,000—a decline of 22%; in 1965 the number of seminarians was 49,000 whereas in 2002 it was 4,700; the percentage of parishes without resident priests rose from 3% in 1965 to 15% in 2002; the number of religious sisters fell from 180,000 to 75,500—half of them 70 or older.

Meanwhile, the number of American Catholics was rising—from 45.6 million (in a total U.S. population of 190 million) in 1965 to 65.3 million (in a population of 285 million) in 2002. All but a tiny fraction, obviously, were lay persons. Except that…were there *really* 65 million Catholics? And "Catholics" in what sense?

It is reasonable to divide Catholics into two large groups: those who are more or less regular about the practice of their faith and those who are not. Sunday Mass attendance is the best measure of religious practice by Catholics. On any given Sunday in the 1960s about 70% of the Catholics in the United States attended Mass. Now, although different studies come up with different results, all agree that the percentage has fallen very substantially. One reasonable estimate is that somewhere between 30% and 40% of American Catholics go to Mass weekly. Another way of putting the matter is to say that in the 1960s two American Catholics out of three attended Sunday Mass, while now only one Catholic in three does that.

The problem doesn't end there. Opinion polls routinely show that huge numbers of American Catholics either do not know what the Church teaches on many important matters or reject that teaching.

In 1999, for example, analysis of a set of opinion surveys sought to track shifts occurring in the attitudes of American Catholics between 1987 and that time. One particularly revealing set of questions asked whether it was possible to be a "good Catholic" in various circumstances: without obeying Church teaching on abortion—39% said yes in 1987, 53% in 1999; and without giving time and money to the poor—44% in 1987, 56% in 1999. Similar majorities said people could be good Catholics without attending Mass on Sunday, without giving time and money to their parishes, and while practicing birth control, divorcing and remarrying, and marrying outside the Church. By 1999, 38% of the Catholics even held that a person could be a good Catholic without believing in Christ's Real Presence in the Eucharist, while 23% took the same view of disbelief in Christ's physical resurrection from the dead.

As everyone knows, the same phenomenon exists in the sphere of political life. In 2004 the pollster John Zogby told an audience at the Catholic University of America he had data showing that American Catholics vote "as veterans, as members of an ethnic group or a union, or according to the region they live in as their primary identity." Their identity as Catholics ranked somewhere farther down the lists as a guide for how they chose to vote. The problem takes an even more acute form in the behavior of Catholic politicians who support legalized abortion, immoral stem cell research, human cloning experimentation, same-sex unions, and the like.

Nominally at least, some dissenting Catholics keep up their link to the Church, but many others don't bother. In the United States the Catholic Church has become what veteran religion writer Kenneth Woodward calls "the farm system for other Christian denominations." Woodward says: "If it weren't for disaffected Catholics, there would be half the number of Episcopalians. Without former Catholics, a lot of local, non-denominational 'community' churches would have to disband, or might not even exist."

Different people react in different ways to all this. But whatever anybody makes of it, it is surely not a picture of a religious community in blooming good health. On the contrary, in the United States and countries like it, Catholicism like the rest of Christianity appears to be in a long-term, continuing state of decline.

It is important to point out, however, that this is how things stand at present in the wealthy, consumerist, highly secularized regions of the world. The situation is very different in the developing countries of the Southern Hemisphere, whether Catholicism and other branches of Christianity are enjoying rapid, even explosive growth.

According to projections, Catholics in Latin America, who numbered 461 million in the year 2000, will total 606 million by 2025; in Africa—120 million in 2000 and 228 million in 2025; in Asia—110 million in 2000 and 160 million in 2025. U.S. and Canadian Catholics will register a comparatively small increase—from 71 million to 81 million—but the Catholic population of Europe is likely to decline—from 286 million in 2000 to 276 million in 2025 (see Philip Jenkins, *The Next Christendom: TheComing of Global Christianity*. New York: Oxford University Press, 2002, page 195). Symbolic of the ongoing North-South shift in Christianity's center of population gravity, Jenkins points out, "there are about half as many Catholics in the whole of the Netherlands as in (say) just the Manila metropolitan area" (*ibid.*, page 198).

In the developing world Catholicism and Christianity in general tend to be traditionalist in doctrine and moral values, and to have pronounced charismatic or Pentecostal streak. The Church in the developing world faces grave problems, of course—dire poverty in many places, a serious shortage of priests, and a disturbing degree of religious syncretism as seen in the emergence of new religious bodies perhaps best described as quasi-Christian—but alongside the problems, there also is great vitality.

Much of this vitality naturally comes from lay people who have stepped forward to do their part as active, engaged members of the Church. As a matter of fact, Jenkins even speculates on the possibility that these "Southern Christians" from the third world will in due course be the ones to re-evangelize the North as immigration brings about large-scale population shifts (*ibid.*, pages 204 ff.).

What Should the Laity Be Doing?

Meanwhile, though, the Church in the United States and in other Western countries is in crisis. The challenge this presents to the Catholic laity is clear. They are called to do more than struggle individually against the temptations that come from the sinful world around them, in hopes of saving their souls (although certainly they need to do that). Lay people also need to shoulder and carry out their part in the mission of the Church, especially in the "*new evangelization*[g]" and the evangelization of culture of which Pope John Paul II spoke of so often.

John Paul returned to this theme in *Novo Millennio Ineunte* ("At the Beginning of the New Millennium"), the Apostolic Letter he published on January 6, 2001, the Feast of the Epiphany, to mark the start of the third millennium of the Christian era. "Even in countries evangelized many centuries ago," he pointed out, "the reality of a 'Christian society'…is now gone."

Rather than being a cause for discouragement, he argued, this troubling state of affairs should provide impetus for a fresh outburst of evangelizing fervor not unlike that of Christianity's early days: "This passion will not fail to stir in the Church a new sense of mission, which cannot be left to a group of 'specialists' but must involve the responsibility of all the members of the People of God....A new apostolic outreach is needed, which will be lived as the everyday commitment of Christian communities and groups" (*Novo Millennio Ineunte*, 40).

The Pope was describing an evangelizing Catholic community, made up overwhelmingly of lay women and men, which in many respects would resemble the Christian community as we glimpsed it earlier in another historic document. Recall the words of the Epistle to Diognetus, written around 200 A.D.: "What the soul is in the body, that the Christians are in the world....Such is the important post to which God has assigned them, and they are not at liberty to desert it." (And we might add: Neither then nor now.)

The practical question is: *How* should lay people respond to these lofty expectations, carry out this most challenging and rewarding role? We already have seen many elements of the answer. Here let us merely recall some things already said, while adding a few other points.

First of all, we need to realize that there are ways for lay people *not* to respond adequately to the need for a new evangelization. Simply ignoring it is one way of course. But so is putting so much emphasis on activities *within* the structures and institutions of the Church—lay ministry, that is—that apostolate in and to the secular world gets short shrift and is virtually ignored.

Several sources support this unhealthy tendency. One of them, ideological in nature, is an updated version of clericalism. Clericalism fosters the idea that the advancement of the laity comes from admitting them to 'ministries' and allowing them to do things (read at Mass, distribute communion, etc.) that only clerics formerly could do. It's like taking children to a fire station and letting them wear the firefighters' hats. The more lay people resemble the clergy in what they do (and even in the way they dress), so it's supposed, the more elevated their status will be.

Another source of the problem is practical rather than ideological. As the number of priests and religious men and women continues to decline, more and more lay people must do work done by clerics and religious in earlier generations in order to make necessary services available and keep ecclesiastical institutions and programs afloat.

True, the emergence of permanent deacons since Vatican Council II has partly alleviated the personnel crunch. (In 2003, there were a little over 14,000 permanent deacons in the United States, a figure which represented nearly half the world total of about 30,000.) But Catholic lay people have provided far more new personnel—both 'lay ministers' serving (mainly in parishes) on a part-time, volunteer basis, and 'lay ecclesial ministers' (also working mostly in parishes, but present also in some other church-related institutions) who usually are full-time, salaried staff. A 1999 study put their number in the United States at 29,145.

For the lay ministers, lay ministry represents a generous impulse on the part of people who want to serve the Church. They are badly needed today in parishes and other settings where there are no longer enough priests, permanent deacons, and religious women and men to go around. But to the extent that this development works hand-in-glove with clericalism to make 'ministry' a preferred *alternative* to lay apostolate in the world, there is urgent need for a change of course.

As has been said here repeatedly, the Second Vatican Council and Pope John Paul II both leave no doubt that the primary role of Catholic lay people in the Church's mission is what traditionally has been called lay apostolate. The faithful, says Vatican II, must "recognize the inner nature, the value and the ordering of the whole of creation to the praise of God."

> By their secular activity they help one another achieve greater holiness of life, so that the world may be filled with the spirit of Christ and may the more effectively attain its destiny in justice, in love and in peace. The laity enjoy a principal role in the universal fulfillment of this task....Thus, through the members of the Church, will Christ increasingly illuminate the whole of human society with his saving light (*Lumen Gentium*, 36).

These are noble words. They will mean very little, however, unless lay people motivated and formed for apostolic work make them reality.

A second mistake that needs to be avoided—or corrected, where it exists—is to reduce the spirituality of the laity to "freedom," as a recent writer does. This one-dimensional emphasis then leads to the suggestion that the sin of Adam and Eve was a good thing after all, something even planned and intended by God, since it marked the start of the mature exercise of human autonomy: "The fall is the true creation of the human world" (Paul Lakeland, *The Liberation of the Laity*. New York: Continuum, 2003, page 179). This is "kneeling before the world" carried to bizarre extremes worthy of that nihilistic herald of the amoral superman, Friedrich Nietzsche (1844-1900).

Having extolled the fall as an exercise of human freedom, the same writer proceeds to envisage the laity's role along lines borrowed from the Marxist-influenced categories of liberation theology. According to this scheme, the current position of the Catholic laity in the United States resembles the degraded position of the proletariat in the Industrial Revolution as Karl Marx and others observed it in the slums of nineteenth century Europe. Thus: "If the vocation of the laity is to human freedom, their existential predicament in today's church is that they are in chains....It is just such a condition of 'structural oppression' that I believe is the present condition of the laity in the church" (*ibid.*, pages 186-187).

Speaking this way trivializes the plight of oppressed people in many places in today's world while also absurdly exaggerating the grievances of middle-class American Catholics. Further opening-up of the decision-making processes in the Church to participation by the laity may indeed be desirable, even necessary, in the Church today; but it is ridiculous to say that, as matters stand, such people are "in chains."

Overemphasizing lay ministry (on the basis of the neo-clericalism that thinks clericalizing the laity leads to their advancement) and arguing for a liberationist view of lay people (as if they were the oppressed urban proletariat of two centuries ago) both are mistakes to avoid. By contrast, the major elements of the path traced here include:

*giving priority to lay apostolate in and to the secular world as the preferred, though not exclusive, form of lay participation in the mission of the Church;

*cultivating an authentically lay spirituality incorporating central elements of lay life and experience like marriage and work;

*discerning, accepting, and living out of the unique personal vocations of lay persons as the essential framework for their apostolate and their personal holiness.

On that basis—but *only* on that basis—progress is possible.

A New Catholic Subculture

This particular puzzle has one other indispensable piece—a new Catholic *subculture*[g] to foster and sustain efforts by Catholic lay people to do these things.

At one time, such a subculture existed in the United States as in other countries. It was the basis upon which the Catholic Church in America, in the middle years of the twentieth century, was on its way to becoming the dominant influence in the shaping of the nation's culture as a whole. In 1944-45 the influential Protestant magazine *The Christian Century* published an eight-part series, "Can Catholicism Win America?" Editor Harold Fey commented that the Catholic Church was committed to "winning the total body of American culture to Catholicism." Conceding that Catholics had a right to do that, Fey added that, without more unity of effort among Protestants, "the answer to the question, Can Catholicism win America? is—yes" (quoted in Charles Morris, *American Catholic*. New York: Times Books, 1997, page 224).

He was right. By the 1950s, "the Church appeared preeminent" (*ibid.*, page 227). But, largely behind the scenes, the dismantling of the Catholic subculture largely responsible for the Church's success had commenced among Catholic academics and intellectuals; it continued throughout the 1960s and 1970s—indeed, it continues to this day.

Factors inside and outside the Church were responsible for what happened. The result was a breakdown of institutional strength and religious identity that, by the start of the twenty-first century, found Catholicism in the United States much weaker in many ways than it had been fifty years earlier. (For an account of what happened, see Morris, *American Catholic*, pages 196-281.)

The conclusion should be obvious. Unless believing, practicing Catholics—in the United States and countries like it, including Canada and the nations of Western Europe—can re-create a strong new Catholic subculture as a basis for their efforts to engage and evangelize the increasingly secularized culture surrounding them, there is virtually no chance that the larger culture will change for the better, but an excellent chance that Catholicism will further decline.

Simply returning to the Catholic subculture of the 1930s, 1940s, and 1950s is not possible, nor would it be desirable if it could be done. Along with its undoubted strengths and virtues, the subculture of that era was triumphalistic, intellectually shallow, and overly defensive. Hardly what is needed now, if the evangelization of culture is the goal.

The new Catholic subculture must instead be built upon an infrastructure of dynamically orthodox institutions, programs, and movements committed to forming and motivating Catholics for the evangelization of the secular world. Here and there, it may be starting to happen. If it is to succeed, lay women and men must play a key role.

Which is simply to say that all members of the Church, all the *Christifideles*, laity, clergy, and religious alike, need to work together to realize the vision presented by Pope John Paul II:

> While this "Christian newness of life" given to the members of the Church constitutes for all the basis of their participation in the priestly, prophetic and kingly mission of Christ and of their vocation to holiness in love, it receives expression and is fulfilled in the lay faithful through the secular character uniquely and properly theirs.... The whole Church, Pastors and lay faithful alike...ought to feel more strongly the Church's responsibility to obey the command of Christ, "Go into all the world and preach the Gospel to the whole creation" (Mk 16:15), and take up anew the missionary endeavor. A great venture, both challenging and wonderful, is entrusted to the Church—that of a re-evangelization, which is so much needed by the present world. The lay faithful ought to regard themselves as an active and responsible part of this venture, called as they are to proclaim and to live the Gospel in service to the person and to society (*Christifideles Laici*, 64).

Spiritual Treasure

The everlasting protest of the world against Christians is that they scorn it, and that by scorning it they misunderstand what constitutes the proper value of its nature: its goodness, its beauty, and its intelligibility. That explains the ceaseless reproaches directed against us, in the name of philosophy, of history, and of science: Christianity refuses to take the whole man, and, under the pretext of making him better, it mutilates him, forcing him to close his eyes to things that constitute the excellence of nature and life, to misunderstand the progress of society throughout history, and to hold suspect science which progressively discloses the laws of nature and those of societies. These reproaches, repeatedly flung at us, are so familiar as to cease to interest us; nevertheless, it is our duty never to cease replying to them, and above all never to lose sight ourselves of what is the reply to them. Yes, Christianity is a radical condemnation of the world, but it is at the same time an unreserved approbation of nature; for the world is not nature, it is nature shaping its course without God.

Etienne Gilson

GLOSSARY

acolyte, from a Greek word for attendant, is an instituted ministry of one who assists the celebrant at Mass. Lay people also can serve at Mass without being installed as acolytes. Women and girls can be altar servers at the discretion of the local bishop.

Ad Gentes—"to the nations"—is the Latin title of the Second Vatican Council's Decree on the Church's Missionary Activity, dated December 7, 1965. It states its focus and scope at the beginning: "Having been divinely sent to the nations that she might be 'the universal sacrament of salvation,' the Church, in obedience to the command of her founder (Mt. 16.15) and because it is demanded by her own essential universality, strives to preach the Gospel to all men."

Apostolicam Actuositatem, "Apostolic Activity," is the Latin title of the Second Vatican Council's Decree on the Apostolate of Lay People, dated November 18, 1965.

Areopagus, the highest judicial council of ancient Athens, also is the name given the public forum where Athenians gathered to exchange news and views. St. Paul's address to the Athenians, delivered in the Areopagus, is reported in the Acts of the Apostles (17.16-34).

Arian heresy, or Arianism, is the belief—originating in the fourth century with an Alexandrian monk named Arius—that Christ was created and therefore was not divine. The heresy was condemned by the Councils of Nicaea (325) and Constantinople (381).

"The Call To Holiness" is the title of Chapter V of the Second Vatican Council's Dogmatic Constitution on the Church *Lumen Gentium*. The chapter sets out the teaching that God intends all members of the Church, including the laity, to achieve sanctity in the circumstances of their particular states in life and vocations.

The key statement is this: "It is therefore quite clear that all Christians in any state or walk of life are called to the fullness of Christian life and to the perfection of love" (n. 40). Chapter V goes on to discuss the sanctity of various groups in the Church and the means to sanctity.

canon is a Greek word meaning rule or measure. In the ecclesiastical context it refers to several things, including a law of the Church or a statement of doctrine or discipline by a Church council or synod; the books of the Bible which the Church recognizes as inspired; the Eucharistic Prayer of the Mass; and a priest who lives at the diocesan cathedral and assists the bishop.

canon law is the law of the Church. In modern times, the first systematic collection of such laws was the Code of Canon Law published in 1917. The revised Code of Canon Law for the Western Church was published in 1983. The Code of Canons of the Eastern Churches appeared in 1990.

Catholic Action is a movement, supported by popes and bishops and particularly strong in the years before the Second Vatican Council, to promote the lay apostolate and form lay people for it. Catholic Action is understood as the participation of the laity in the apostolate of the hierarchy.

Catholic Worker, founded by Dorothy Day (1897-1980) and Peter Maurin (1877-1949), is a lay movement that serves the poor in "houses of hospitality" and other settings and promotes a radical vision of Christianity including voluntary poverty and pacifism. The Catholic Worker and the example of Dorothy Day had considerable influence on Catholic intellectuals and lay activists in the United States in the 1940s and 1950s.

Centesimus Annus, "The Hundredth Year," is an encyclical on social doctrine published by Pope John Paul II in 1991. The title refers to the centenary of Pope Leo XIII's groundbreaking social encyclical *Rerum Novarum*, published in 1891. In *Centesimus*

Annus Pope John Paul discusses the social teaching of the Church in light of circumstances following the fall of communism in 1989.

charity, with faith and hope, is one of the three supernaturally infused "theological" virtues and is considered the highest one. It refers to habitual love of God and love of self and neighbor for God's sake.

christifideles is a Latin word meaning Christ's faithful people. It is the general term for all members of the Church, both laity and clergy. The Latin name of Pope John Paul II's Post-Synodal Apostolic Exhortation on the laity, published in 1989, is *Christifideles Laici*—The Lay Members of Christ's Faithful People.

cleric is the term for members of the Church who are in Holy Orders. Bishops, priests, and deacons are clerics.

clericalism historically is a term referring to over-involvement by the clergy in politics and temporal affairs generally. Currently the term is used in a more general sense, to refer to a mindset which considers the clerical state to be normative for other Christian states in life and views the clergy as the active element in the life of the Church and the laity as the passive element.

clericalization refers to a process whose effect is to isolate clerics from the laity and assign them a superior position in the Church while encouraging lay people to be passive and more or less disengaged from the Church's mission.

cloning is the artificial production of genetically identical organisms from the original organism. The cloning of human beings, whether for reproductive, experimental or allegedly therapeutic purposes, is condemned by the Catholic Church. See, for example, the Congregation for the Doctrine of the Faith's *Instruction on Respect for Human Life in Its Origin and on the Dignity of Procreation: Replies to Certain Questions of the Day, Donum Vitae* (1987).

Cluniac reform is the name for the tenth- and eleventh-century reform movement in the Church which arose at the Benedictine monastery of Cluny in France and spread through Europe. It stressed the reform of monastic life and clerical life generally.

commitment is a large, life-determining choice requiring many implementing choices to carry it out. It is more a decision to be something than to do something. Typical commitments are the choice of a state in life, a career or occupation, a marriage partner, etc.

communio ecclesiology is the theology of the Church associated with Vatican Council II; it emphasizes the Church's communal nature and structure mirroring the communio of the Trinity and leading to communio among local churches and members of the Church. 'Body of Christ' and 'People of God' are images of the Church that express an ecclesiology of communion.

Congregation for the Doctrine of the Faith is the office or "dicastery" of the Holy See responsible for promoting orthodox doctrine. Established in its present form by Pope Paul VI in 1965, it previously was called the Holy Office. Its origins date back to the thirteenth century.

congregationalism is the view, embodied in a form of Protestantism, that each group or congregation of Christian believers is autonomous in governance. In regard to worship, congregationalism holds that it is the congregation as a group which worships, while those who preside, rather than being priests in the Catholic sense, simply organize and direct the congregational action.

consecrated life, like religious life, is a Christian lifestyle characterized by the practice of the evangelical counsels (poverty, chastity, obedience); however, the term includes not only men and women religious but others—e.g., lay members of secular institutes and other apostolic groups—who do not belong to religious institutes and may not take vows.

contemptus mundi is Latin for "contempt of the world." The term refers to rejection of the temptations and false allurements of the world as it is marred by sin. But it is also sometimes identified with an overemphasis on negative elements present in the world which fails to recognize the secular order as a sphere for Christian action.

Council of Ephesus, the third ecumenical council, took place at Ephesus in Asia Minor in 431 AD. It is best known for declaring that the Virgin Mary is rightly called *theotokos* (Greek: Mother of God). This is important not only as a matter of Marian doctrine but in regard to doctrine about Christ.

courtship is a vocational discernment by which a man and woman discern whether it is God's will that they marry each other. Practically speaking, it is a sort of extended conversation through which the couple get to know each other as they truly are and share their views on questions of faith and morality as well as everyday matters. Consultation with others—parents, friends, spiritual advisors—is part of it. If the couple decide God wants them to marry each other, the courtship ends and is followed by engagement, the immediate preparation for marriage.

culture is described by the Second Vatican Council as follows: "The word 'culture' in the general sense refers to all those things which go to the refining and developing of man's diverse mental and physical endowments" (Pastoral Constitution on the Church in the Modern World, *Gaudium et Spes,* n. 53). The Council says contemporary culture has been characterized by "tremendous expansion" in science, technology, and the media of communication, with profound consequences for human life.

Culture of Death is the name given by Pope John Paul II to the collection of anti-life ideologies and forces in the contemporary world. He contrasts it with what he calls the Culture of Life. The nature, sources, and components of the Culture of Death are discussed at length in his 1995 encyclical *Evangelium Vitae* ("The Gospel of Life") and other writings.

cultural assimilation is a psychological and sociological process by which members of a group adopt the beliefs, attitudes, values, patterns of behavior, institutions, etc. of the surrounding culture and are integrated into it.

deregulation is the name for a government policy of removing or relaxing controls over an industry or industry sector, in order to encourage free enterprise and competition. In the United States deregulation has been applied in various ways to utilities, transportation, banking, and communications, especially the broadcast media.

diaconate is the name for the order of deacon, which along with the priesthood and the episcopate is one of the three divisions within the sacrament of Orders. Deacons are of two kinds: permanent deacons, who remain deacons, and transitional deacons, for whom the diaconate is a stage on the way to priestly ordination.

dialectic in general refers to the process by which one idea or state of affairs gives rise to another idea or state of affairs more or less opposed to it. There are well known dialectical systems associated with the philosophers Hegel and Marx.

Episcopal conference is the assembly of bishops of a particular country or region through which they collaborate in reaching decisions and carrying out joint programs in their areas of pastoral responsibility. Vatican II recommended episcopal conferences in *Lumen Gentium* and *Christus Dominus*, and they are recognized in canon law. After the Council the American bishops created a dual structure, the National Conference of Catholic Bishops and the United States Catholic Conference; in 1997 these were reorganized into a unitary structure called the United States Conference of Catholic Bishops. It has headquarters in Washington, D.C. Pope John Paul II published an important Apostolic Letter on "the theological and juridical nature of episcopal conferences," *Apostolos Suos,* in 1998.

Escriva, St. Josemaria, founder of Opus Dei, was born in Barbastro, Spain, January 9, 1902, and died in Rome June 26, 1975. Pope John Paul II declared him a saint on October 6, 2002. Monsignor Escriva founded Opus Dei in Madrid on October 2, 1928, as a way of sanctification for persons living and working in the world. He lived in Rome directing its growth and development from 1946 until his death.

evangelical counsels is the name for poverty, chastity, and obedience. Members of institutes of consecrated life commit themselves by vows or promises to the practice of the counsels; but all Christians should live by the spirit of the counsels according to their states in life and personal vocations.

Evangelii Nuntiandi is the Latin title of Pope Paul VI's Apostolic Exhortation "On Evangelization in the Modern World." Responding to the 1974 world Synod of Bishops on this theme, the document presents a comprehensive vision of and rationale for evangelization, situates it at the heart of the Church's mission, and makes it clear that participation in preaching the gospel is a right and duty of all members of the Church.

evangelization is the proclamation of the Gospel, the "Good News," with the aim of converting the hearers to faith in Christ or, in the case of those already Christians, to deeper faith; evangelization is central to the mission of the Church and to apostolate, and is done both by witness of life and by specific proclamation.

evangelization of culture is a term often used by Pope John Paul II to describe the process of infusing Christian values into the structures important cultural institutions such as the universities and the communication media. See, for example, *Christifideles Laici,* n. 44.

Familiaris Consortio, also known as *The Family in the Modern World*, is Pope John Paul II's 1981 Apostolic Exhortation in response to the 1980 world synod of bishops on the family. The document discusses the situation of the family in today's world, God's plan for the family, the role of the Christian family, and pastoral care of families.

formation, a broader concept than education, refers to promoting and guiding the development of persons in their spiritual and ascetical aspects as well as in their intellectual growth. Formation is central to the preparation of candidates for the priesthood and consecrated life as well as lay ministries and lay apostolates, and is an ongoing requirement for all members of the Church.

Gaudium et Spes, "Joy and Hope," is the Latin title of the Second Vatican Council's Pastoral Constitution on the Church in the Modern World, dated December 7, 1965.

Great Depression is the name for a worldwide economic downturn in the 1930s. In the United States and other countries the stock market crashed, many people lost their savings, many business enterprises collapsed, and there was high unemployment, much poverty, and widespread social unrest.

Holy Orders, or simply Orders, is one of the seven sacraments. It includes three orders or divisions: diaconate, priesthood, and episcopate. Ordination is the sacramental act, administered by a bishop, by which a man, becomes a member of one of these orders.

Human rights refer to the collection of entitlements thought to belong to human beings by nature. Referring to the United Nations Declaration of Human Rights (1948) and Pope John XXIII's encyclical *Pacem in Terris* (1963), Pope John Paul II speaks of a "more lively sense of human rights" since World War II, and adds: "Not only has there been a development in awareness of individuals, but also in awareness of the rights of nations" (*Centesimus Annus*, n. 21).

humanism is a school of thought emphasizing human beings and human concerns. Secular humanism is a form of atheism, either theoretical or practical, that stresses the human apart from God: e.g., Marxism. Christian humanism focuses on the human within the context of faith.

Immaculate Conception is the doctrine that the Virgin Mary was preserved "free from all stain of original sin" from the first instant of her conception. It was solemnly defined as a dogma of Catholic faith by Blessed Pope Pius IX on December 8, 1854.

The Imitation of Christ is a famous spiritual work attributed to Thomas à Kempis (c. 1380-1471) and published in 1472. It is said that among religious books, only the Bible is more widely read. The volume has helped generations of Christians in their pursuit of sanctity and remains of great value today, but it reflects a negative view of the world and prospects for holiness there. In a more general sense, "the imitation of Christ" is the fundamental enterprise of Christian life—to conform one's life in its entirety to the model of Christ.

in persona Christi (or, *in persona Christi capitis*) is a Latin phrase meaning in the person of Christ (or, in the person of Christ the Head). It refers to the unique role of the ordained priest, who, in celebrating the sacraments and performing other functions proper to his ministerial role, performs actions that are essentially actions of Christ himself.

International Theological Commission is a body of scholars established by Pope Paul VI in 1969 to serve in an advisory capacity to the Vatican's Congregation for the Doctrine of the Faith. It meets yearly, with the prefect of that congregation presiding, and has produced a number of documents on important theological topics.

The Introduction to the Devout Life is the title of an immensely popular spiritual classic by St. Francis de Sales (1567-1622). It was published in 1609. The book provides guidance to persons seeking to lead holy lives in the world and deals with matters like prayer, the sacraments, and the practice of the virtues.

Laborem Exercens ("engaging in work") is the Latin title of an encyclical published by Pope John Paul II in 1981. Appearing on the 90th anniversary of Pope Leo XIII's social encyclical *Rerum Novarum,* the document discusses human work in relation to social justice, the dignity of the person, and spirituality.

laicism is a term for the anticlerical movement which arose in Europe in the eighteenth and nineteenth centuries in opposition to clericalism. It is strongly ideological and political. Laicism is the immediate ancestor of many efforts directed to the secularization of society today.

laity, from the Greek word *laos* ("people"), is the name for the members of the Church who are not in Holy Orders. Today the term *Christifideles laici* (the lay members of Christ's faithful) is sometimes used.

lay apostolate is the participation of the laity in the mission of the Church. In Catholic Action, the right to participate comes to lay people by delegation from the hierarchy. Vatican Council II says the fundamental right and duty to participate in apostolate, both individual and group, come to the laity from Christ through baptism and confirmation.

lay investiture was the medieval practice according to which lay lords conferred office upon holders of Church offices—bishops, abbots, parish priests. Lay investiture was the focus of a long and sometimes bitter struggle between ecclesiastical authorities and temporal authorities.

lay ministry, strictly speaking, includes the liturgical roles of lector, acolyte, and cantor. Lay people also can be commissioned as extraordinary ministers of communion. In recent years, 'lay ministry' frequently has been used as a catchall term for many different service roles performed by lay people in parishes and other church settings.

lay trusteeism was a system that began in places in the United States in the late eighteenth century and continued until the mid-nineteenth century and involved the ownership of parish property by Catholic laymen, who decided many Church matters. Trusteeism was opposed by the bishops and condemned by Pope Pius VII in 1822.

lector, Latin for reader, is the name of the formally instituted ministry of one who does the Scripture readings (except for the gospel) during the liturgy. The ministry of lector is reserved to men, but lay people, both women and men, also can serve as readers without being installed in the ministry of lector.

liberation theology is a theological movement, identified especially with Latin America, which focuses upon the empowerment of the poor and, to some extent, uses categories derived from a Marxist analysis of social problems. It is critiqued in two documents published by the Vatican's Congregation for the Doctrine of the Faith in 1984 and 1986.

liturgical movement was the movement for the reform and renewal of the Catholic liturgy that flourished in the first half of the twentieth century and exercised an influence on Vatican Council II. Its emphasis on lay participation in the Mass and on the liturgy as foundation and source of Catholic social action links it to Catholic Action and the lay apostolate.

liturgy is the public worship of the Church. The celebration of the Eucharist is the preeminent liturgical act.

Lumen Gentium, "The Light of Nations," is the Latin title of the Second Vatican Council's Dogmatic Constitution on the Church, dated November 21, 1964.

Magisterium is a Latin name for the teaching authority of the Church, instituted by Christ and exercised under the direction of the Holy Spirit. This teaching authority is present in the Pope and the bishops in union with him.

Maritain, Jacques (1882-1973), a French Catholic philosopher, was a leading figure in the revival of the philosophy of St. Thomas Aquinas. Maritain lived and taught for many years in the United States. His books include *The Degrees of Knowledge, Creative Intuition in Art and Poetry, Integral Humanism, The Peasant of the Garonne*, and many others.

media education refers to the training of audiences of media—readers, viewers, listeners—intended to familiarize them with how media operate and help them to be more sophisticated and selective in their use of media. Media education is frequently recommended in documents of the Church dealing with the media of social communication.

mediation, as a religious concept, refers to the fact that, besides dealing directly and 'immediately' with human beings, God commonly acts through others (especially priestly 'mediators,' among whom Jesus Christ is supreme and unique) and through religious actions and objects, especially the Mass and the sacraments.

ministry is the name for a role of service in the Church, modeled on the threefold office of Christ as priest, teacher, and king. Ministry properly so called belongs to clerics, but in a more general sense the term also refers to service roles performed within the Church by lay people. Ministry is a formally instituted office of service within the Church, often of a liturgical nature. Ministries properly so called pertain only to the ordained; roles of service assigned to non-ordained persons are called ministries in an analogical sense.

mission comes from a Latin word meaning "to send." In general terms, a mission is a body of persons sent to convey a message to others or negotiate with them; it also refers to the task entrusted to them or to some individual. The Church's mission, assigned to it by Christ and generically called "the apostolate," is to preach the gospel. All members of the Church are called to participate in this work by reason of their baptismal vocation, but how individuals should do that depends on their state in life and personal vocation. In popular speech, a "missionary" is someone who carries the gospel to people who have not heard it, often in a remote area.

monasticism is a way of life emphasizing withdrawal from the world for the practice of prayer and penance, either alone or in community with others. Monasticism arose in the East with St. Anthony in the fourth century and in the West with St. Benedict in the sixth century.

More, St. Thomas (1478-1535), Lord Chancellor of England from 1529 to 1532, was executed by King Henry VIII for his opposition to the King's divorce from Catherine of Aragon and to Henry's claim of supremacy over the Church in England. He was canonized in 1935. He is the author of numerous literary works, including *Utopia.*

Mystical Body of Christ is a name for the Church stressing its unique unity with Christ, as well as the fundamental equality of the members within a hierarchical structure in which all have complementary roles. The term originates in the writings of St. Paul. The Church as Mystical Body of Christ is the subject of an important encyclical of Pope Pius XII, *Mystici Corporis*, published in 1943, and is one of the images used by the Second Vatican Council (1962-65) to express the mystery of the Church in the first chapter of its Dogmatic Constitution, *Lumen Gentium.*

National Pastoral Council is a national-level body of bishops, clergy, religious, and laity exercising shared responsibility in designated areas of the Church's life, especially matters pertaining to political and social policy. Steps toward the creation of such a body were taken in the United States in the 1960s and 1970s, but the effort eventually was abandoned and the subject is rarely discussed these days. In *Christifideles Laici* Pope John Paul II says national conferences of bishops should seek "the most opportune way of developing the consultation and the collaboration of the lay faithful, women and men, at a national or regional level" (n. 25).

neocongregationalism refers to a contemporary school of theological thought which reduces or eliminates the distinction between ordained and non-ordained ministry and tends toward the elimination of hierarchical structure in the Church.

new evangelization is a term often used by Pope John Paul II to describe the preaching of the Gospel anew to societies (e.g., in Western Europe) that were identifiably Christian in earlier times but in recent centuries have become largely secularized and detached from their Christian roots.

Opus Dei (Latin: the work of God) is a predominantly lay organization founded in 1928 to help people who live and work in the world achieve sanctity in ordinary life. It places special emphasis on work and apostolate along with traditional practices of Catholic spirituality. In canonical terms, Opus Dei is a personal prelature, a form of ecclesiastical jurisdiction with a bishop as prelate, whose faithful are the members of Opus Dei itself. At this time, Opus Dei has more than 80,000 members, both men and women and including about 2,000 priests. The members represent some 80 nationalities.

original sin is the sin of the first human persons (Adam and Eve: cf. Gen. 2.8-3.24). For them, it was a personal sin, which they committed. For their descendants, it is a state of alienation from God and privation of sanctifying grace, accompanied by a 'wounding' of human nature and a weakening of natural human powers, called concupiscence, that disposes people to commit personal sins of their own. The state of original sin, but not its effects, is removed by baptism.

Pastores Dabo Vobis—I will give you shepherds (cf. Jer 3.15)—is the Latin title of Pope John Paul II's post-synodal apostolic exhortation on "the formation of priests in the circumstances of the present day." Dated March 25, 1992, it is his response to the eighth ordinary general assembly of the world Synod of Bishops, which met in 1990.

Percy, Walker (1916-1990), a physician by training, was a novelist and convert to Catholicism. His first novel, *The Moviegoer* (1961), won the National Book Award. Other works include *Love in the Ruins* (1971) and *The Thanatos Syndrome* (1987). He also published articles and books on philosophical subjects.

personalism is a philosophical school or orientation that emphasizes the centrality of the human person in philosophical reflection. Christian personalism stresses the dignity of the person understood in the light of Christ. It is associated with the French Catholic philosopher Gabriel Marcel and with the Polish "Lublin school" to which Karol Wojtyla—Pope John Paul II—belonged.

priesthood of the faithful, also called the common priesthood or baptismal priesthood, is the doctrine that, in virtue of baptism, all Christians participate in the mission of Christ, which is also the Church's mission, of sanctifying, teaching, and ruling. The priesthood of the faithful and the ministerial, ordained priesthood differ essentially and not just in degree. (See *Lumen Gentium* 10-12.)

Redemptoris Missio (The Mission of the Redeemer) is the Latin title of Pope John Paul II's 1990 encyclical "On the Permanent Validity of the Church's Missionary Mandate." Published to mark the 25th anniversary of *Ad Gentes*, Vatican II's Decree on the Church's Missionary Activity, the encyclical calls for a universal commitment to evangelization on the part of Catholics.

Reformation is the name for the sixteenth- and seventh-century movement that divided Western Christianity into those in union with the Holy See, who subscribed to traditional formulas of faith and forms of religious practice, and those in other bodies, commonly called Protestant, who rejected papal authority and adopted new expressions of religious faith and practice. The Reformation began with Martin Luther (1483-1546). The Catholic response, called the Counter-Reformation, is associated especially with the Council of Trent (1545-1563).

religious life, a state in life in which men and women seek perfection and, often, carry on a variety of apostolates in communities whose members take solemn vows of poverty, chastity, and obedience. Vatican Council II's decree *Perfectae Caritatis* (October 28, 1965) discusses the renewal of religious life.

Salvifici Doloris, "Salvific Suffering," is an Apostolic Letter "on the Christian meaning of human suffering" published by Pope John Paul II in 1984.

secular: of or pertaining to the world and the things of the world, in contrast with other-worldly or spiritual. To say something is secular does not express approval or disapproval, but only states a sociological fact.

secularism is an ideology or system of belief which assigns an absolute priority to worldly matters over spiritual ones; militant secularism, frequently atheistic, seeks to exclude religion and religious interests from public life.

secularization is the social process by which secularism emerges and tends to become dominant in a society; secularization has spread rapidly in Western society in recent centuries.

shared responsibility refers to the idea that non-bishops—priests, deacons, religious, and laity—can collaborate in appropriate ways with bishops in decision-making in the Church. The concept is grounded in the Second Vatican Council's teaching on the Church and the roles of its members, as found in documents like *Lumen Gentium* and *Apostolicam Actuositatem.* Since Vatican II, shared responsibility has been expressed through bodies like parish and diocesan councils. The expression "coresponsibility" also is sometimes used, but it is subject to misinterpretation.

Soviet Union is a name for the Union of Soviet Socialist Republics established after the Communist takeover following the Russian Revolution of 1917. The USSR was officially atheistic. It was a federation of 15 republics, including the Russian, the Ukrainian, the Byelorussian, and others. The Soviet Union formally dissolved December 26, 1991, with its constituent republics becoming independent nations.

spiritual reading is a traditional part of a spiritual program or plan of life involving regular reading of helpful works by recognized spiritual masters—e.g., *The Imitation of Christ*, *The Introduction to the Devout Life* by St. Francis de Sales, the autobiography of St. Teresa of Avila, *The Story of a Soul* by St. Thérèse of Lisieux, the homilies of Cardinal Newman, *The Way* by St. Josemaria Escriva, etc. Saints' lives by recognized authors also typically are part of spiritual reading.

spirituality refers to the system or approach by which a person seeks to establish, maintain, and deepen his or her relationship with God. For a Christian, spirituality is always focused especially on Christ and the attempt to model one's life on his; it involves liturgical and personal prayer, frequent reception of the sacraments, especially Penance and the Eucharist, the reading of Scripture, and other practices. There are various 'schools' of spirituality in the Catholic tradition: Salesian, Ignatian, etc. In recent times a specifically lay spirituality appropriate to lay persons living in the world has emerged.

state in life is the term for a recognized category of membership in the Church, characterized by a vocational calling, discernment, commitment, and the living-out of the obligations and rights of the state. The clerical state, consecrated life centering on the practice of poverty, chastity, and obedience, marriage, and the single life in the world are states in life. Vatican II says "all Christians in any state or walk of life are called to the fullness of Christian life and to the perfection of love" (*Lumen Gentium* 40).

subculture is a sociological term for a set of institutions, customs, values, etc. shared by members of a particular group identifiable on the basis of religion, ethnicity, or some other factor or combination of factors, and existing in the context of a larger, dominant culture.

Synod of Bishops, a consultative body recommended by the Second Vatican Council to collaborate with the pope. Representative bishops from around the world and officials of the Roman Curia are convened by the pope to advise him on topics he designates. Synod assemblies can be ordinary, extraordinary, or regional. The first assembly of the Synod was held in 1967; through 2005 there had been eleven ordinary assemblies and two extraordinary assemblies, as well as a number of regional or special assemblies.

tonsure is the practice originating in monastic life of shaving some or all of the hair from the head.

Veritatis Splendor, "The Splendor of Truth," is the Latin title of Pope John Paul II's 1993 encyclical on moral principles. Addressed to the Pope's brother bishops, the encyclical, John Paul's tenth, is a carefully reasoned defense of the truth of absolute moral norms and other fundamental elements of the moral life against relativizing theories which deny them.

vocation, from the Latin *vocatio*, "a calling." In a general sense, vocation refers to a profession or career. In religious terms, a vocation is God's calling to an individual to make a commitment to a particular way of life or comprehensive program of Christian activity.

vocational discernment is the process by which an individual or group comes to see and make a commitment to God's will in regard to some large, life-determining matter. Involving prayer and reflection and consultation with a spiritual guide and, often, trusted friends, it is carried out in fidelity to the teaching of the Church and in obedience to legitimate religious authority.

About the Author

Russell Shaw is author or co-author of sixteen previous books, including *To Hunt, To Shoot, To Entertain: Clericalism and the Catholic Laity* (Ignatius Press, 1993), *Papal Primacy in the Third Millennium* (Our Sunday Visitor, 2000), and, with Germain Grisez, *Personal Vocation: God Calls Everyone By Name* (Our Sunday Visitor, 2003). Shaw is editor of *Our Sunday Visitor's Encyclopedia of Catholic Doctrine* (1997) and a contributing editor of *Crisis* and *Columbia* magazines. He was the director of information for the National Conference of Catholic Bishops/United States Catholic Conference from 1969 to 1987 and of the Knights of Columbus from 1987 to 1997. He is a consultor of the Pontifical Council for Social Communications and teaches at the Pontifical University of the Holy Cross, Rome. He and his wife have five children and nine grandchildren.